NATIONAL SECURITY RESEARCH DIVISION

T0302703

Return and Expand?

The Finances and Prospects of the Islamic State After the Caliphate

Patrick B. Johnston, Mona Alami, Colin P. Clarke, Howard J. Shatz

For more information on this publication, visit www.rand.org/t/RR3046

Library of Congress Cataloging-in-Publication Data is available for this publication.
ISBN: 978-1-9774-0319-3

Published by the RAND Corporation, Santa Monica, Calif.

Cover: Getty Images

Preface

As of March 2019, the Islamic State had been ejected from its territorial holdings in Iraq and Syria after having conquered an area the size of Great Britain. But the end of its territorial caliphate does not necessarily mean the end of the group. Understanding the future of the Islamic State requires an assessment of its finances. This report provides details on the many ways the group has raised money and spent money and offers an assessment of what the group's financial activities mean for its likelihood to reemerge. Throughout its history, the Islamic State and its predecessor groups have focused on raising money locally. With this money, it has conducted a wide range of terrorist and military operations and even run a state, at least for a short time.

The Islamic State will almost certainly attempt a comeback. To fund this effort, the group will go with what has consistently worked for it in the past: diversifying revenue sources to maintain steady access to financing and raising money locally. The Islamic State's knack for fundraising through criminal activities will prove useful, as will the likelihood that it has information on the many millions of people who once lived under its rule. In addition, it appears to have sizable assets in reserve. As an insurgency, rather than a territorial government, its expenses are also far lower than they were at the peak of its power. Controlling territory would facilitate these activities but is not a prerequisite. Accordingly, the United States will need to stay involved with counter–Islamic State activities across several lines of effort, including countering the group's revenue-raising activities and potentially including military action.

This research was sponsored by the Smith Richardson Foundation and conducted within the International Security and Defense Policy Center of the RAND National Security Research Division (NSRD). NSRD conducts research and analysis for the Office of the Secretary of Defense, the Joint Staff, the Unified Combatant Commands, the defense agencies, the Navy, the Marine Corps, the U.S. Coast Guard, the U.S. Intelligence Community, allied foreign governments, and foundations.

For more information on the International Security and Defense Policy Center, see www.rand.org/nsrd/ndri/centers/isdp or contact the director (contact information is provided on the webpage).

Contents

Tables

Summary

The Islamic State gained billions of dollars in revenue this decade, using this money to conquer territory, establish a self-styled caliphate, rule over a population of millions, and amass an army that conducted deadly terrorist operations throughout the Middle East and the world. As of March 2019, a multinational campaign against it had destroyed the territorial caliphate, with the last battle led by the Syrian Democratic Forces against Islamic State holdouts in Baghouz, Syria. And yet reports of Islamic State activity in many parts of Iraq and Syria continue to emerge. And it continues to raise revenue. Reports vary, but as of early 2019, it may have held the equivalent of more than $400 million in assets.

Understanding the future of the Islamic State requires an assessment of its finances. Throughout its history, the Islamic State and its predecessor groups have focused on raising money locally. With this money, they have conducted a wide range of terrorist and military operations and reemerged from apparent defeat.

The Islamic State will certainly try to reemerge from this defeat. Without ongoing actions across numerous dimensions—law enforcement, intelligence, economic reconstruction, military, and political—the group could succeed. Should such a return occur, the group will likely retain its underlying structure, methods of operating, and goals, as it has throughout its long existence under different names. An Islamic State slogan during the time of its territorial caliphate was "remaining and expanding." Now, the question is whether the group will return and expand.

Ideology, Strategy, and Organization

The Islamic State's ideology, strategy, and organizational structure all contribute to the group's culture and operational and tactical behavior, which in turn directly affect and are supported by the group's financial behavior and economic decisionmaking. The Islamic State has gone through a variety of iterations. Its original core came from a group called Jama'at al-Tawhid wal-Jihad that was founded in the 1990s by a Jordanian terrorist and fighter called Abu Musab al-Zarqawi. Under Zarqawi's leadership in Iraq, the group then aligned with al-Qa'ida in October 2004, forming al-Qa'ida in Iraq, short for the true name it adopted, The Organization of the Base of Jihad in Mesopotamia. In January 2006, it organized the formation of an umbrella group called the Mujahideen Shura Council. In October 2006, eight years before the group stormed into Mosul, Iraq, it declared the establishment of the Islamic State of Iraq (ISI) and named a *commander of the faithful*, a title historically reserved for Islamic caliphs.

From mid-2007 through 2011, the group was on the defensive and near defeat. During that period, its top leaders were killed, and it was ejected from its openly held territory. But even as late as 2011, some analysts noted that the group's structure and ability to generate local funding and recruits could keep it as an effective fighting force.

With the onset of the civil war in Syria, ISI established a new group in that country but declined to claim any affiliation. In 2013, ISI established an overt presence in Syria and the leadership renamed the group the Islamic State in Iraq and Syria (ISIS; also known as the Islamic State in Iraq and al-Sham, or the Islamic State in Iraq and the Levant [ISIL]). In early 2014, al-Qa'ida disavowed the group, whereupon ISIS became a fully independent entity. Finally, after the June 2014 conquest of Mosul, ISIS renamed itself the Islamic State and deemed its leader, Abu Bakr al-Baghdadi, its first caliph, the Caliph Ibrahim.

Throughout its history, the Islamic State has consistently attempted to forge a reputation among Sunni Muslims, members of the majority branch of Islam, that it represents the purest form of Islam and that it is their protector, while also directing vitriol toward Shia Muslims, part of its sectarian agenda. The group has held long-term plans for establishing a territorial state, including defining substate boundaries, and maintained a bureaucratic blueprint for running the organization that enables it not only to conduct operations but also to cultivate new top officials when its leadership is killed.

Since its inception, the Islamic State has held a consistent financial strategy that aims to support and advance the group's broader religious and state-building goals. The Islamic State's financial strategy and doctrine are characterized by three facets: The group strives to be self-sufficient financially; derives its basic rules and governance of the economy from Islamic economic principles; and, despite these principles, maintains the capacity for significant adaptability and resilience to changing circumstances, battlefield environments, and economic shocks, sometimes deviating from its basic principles to ensure its survival as an organization and its ability to wage jihad in service to its state-building goals.

Islamic State Revenue

The Islamic State has always had a diversified revenue stream. At its peak during the time of the territorial caliphate, this likely amounted to $1 billion or $2 billion (or more) in a year (Table S.1). There have been two consistent patterns to Islamic State revenue raising. First has been an effort to raise money from local sources rather than relying on external donations. Second has been creative diversification. When it controlled territory, it earned revenue from the oil and gas fields it controlled, from taxing and fining the local population, from selling antiquities, and from taxing transit, among other sources. When it did not control territory, it carried out what can be considered criminal activity, including extorting contracts, demanding protection money, and stealing and reselling goods, among other activities.

This diversification of sources comes through clearly in interviews with people who lived under Islamic State rule. In the realm of oil-related revenue, the group sold oil within Islamic State territory but also through traders to the Bashar al-Assad regime and liberated areas in Syria, Kurdish areas, and even Iraq and Turkey. For a fee, it licensed

Table S.1
Estimated Islamic State Revenues, by Year, U.S. $ Millions

Year	Low	Medium	High
2014	970	1,890	2,900
2015	1,035	1,700	2,400
2016	520	870	870
2017	192	192	192

SOURCES: Adam Szubin, "Remarks by Acting Under Secretary Adam Szubin at Chatham House," Washington, D.C.: U.S. Department of the Treasury, December 10, 2015; Daniel Glaser, "Testimony of A\S for Terrorist Financing Daniel Glaser Before the House Committee on Foreign Affairs Subcommittee on Terrorism, Nonproliferation, and Trade and the House Committee on Armed Services, Subcommittee on Emerging Threats and Capabilities," Washington, D.C.: U.S. Department of the Treasury, June 9, 2016b; Yaya J. Fanusie and Alex Entz, "Islamic State Financial Assessment," Washington, D.C.: Foundation for Defense of Democracies, Center on Sanctions and Illicit Finance, March 2017; Stefan Heißner, Peter R. Neumann, John Holland-McCowan, and Rajan Basra, "Caliphate in Decline: An Estimate of Islamic State's Financial Fortunes," London: International Centre for the Study of Radicalisation, 2017; IHS Markit, "Islamic State Monthly Revenue Drops to $56 Million, IHS Says," press release, April 18, 2016; IHS Markit, "Islamic State Territory Down 60 Percent and Revenue Down 80 Percent on Caliphate's Third Anniversary, IHS Markit Says," press release, June 29, 2017; Erika Solomon, Guy Chazan, and Sam Jones, "ISIS Inc.: How Oil Fuels the Jihadi Terrorists," *Financial Times*, October 14, 2015; Erika Solomon and Sam Jones, "ISIS Inc.: Loot and Taxes Keep Jihadi Economy Churning," *Financial Times*, December 14, 2015; Sarah Almukhtar, "ISIS Finances Are Strong," *New York Times*, May 19, 2015; Jean-Charles Brisard and Damien Martinez, *Islamic State: The Economy-Based Terrorist Funding*, ThomsonReuters Accelus, October 2014; Laurence Bindner and Gabriel Poirot, *ISIS Financing in 2015*, Paris: Center for the Analysis of Terrorism, May 2016; Colin P. Clarke, Kimberly Jackson, Patrick B. Johnston, Eric Robinson, Howard J. Shatz, *Financial Futures of the Islamic State of Iraq and the Levant: Findings from a RAND Corporation Workshop*, Santa Monica, Calif.: RAND Corporation, CF-361, 2017; Financial Action Task Force, *Financing of the Terrorist Organization Islamic State in Iraq and the Levant*, Paris, 2015.

NOTES: Various sources were consulted to provide a generic overview from extant reporting of Islamic State revenue trends over time across three categories of revenue estimates: a low, a medium, and a high estimate. The low is the lowest reported believable number; the high is the highest reported believable number; and the medium is a reported, in-between number.

the operation of oil fields. Oil was not the only resource in the ground. It also considered antiquities a resource and licensed people to find, excavate, smuggle, and sell antiquities.

Among nonoil revenues, it levied *zakah* or *zakat*, an Islamic tax requiring payment of 2.5 percent of net worth. In doing so, it required people to inform the Islamic State of their properties so that the group could calculate taxes owed. It recorded income in registers and inspected people's property. There were other taxes and fees, including taxes on money transfers; transit taxes on vehicles entering or leaving its territories; fees for municipal services, such as cleaning; the rental of stalls in markets; and fees for utilities, such as electricity, water, and telephone service. As the purveyor of its own form of justice, the group also collected money through fines for violations of its interpretation of Islamic law.

The Islamic State also gained substantial revenues from confiscations. It took an estimated $500 million or more from banks in northern and western Iraq. But confiscations were not merely confined to money. The group confiscated factories, houses (especially those owned by religious minorities), equipment from hospitals, farm animals, and other items.

The Islamic State's business model after the territorial caliphate will still enable it to raise revenue. In the years from 2004 through 2014, with striking similarities to an organized criminal enterprise, it earned money through smuggling, especially of oil at one point; protection rackets; contract skimming; theft and resale of everything from pajamas to real estate; and other activities. Although these sources included donations, the group's records show that donations were never a large share of total revenues, demonstrating that the group had a strong ability to raise money through a diversified local revenue stream. By 2014, before the group made its major territorial expansion, it was estimated to have the equivalent of $875 million in assets.

With the end of the territorial caliphate, the most pernicious consequence of having held territory is that the Islamic State collected records on the individuals over which it ruled. Given its record-keeping practices, it is likely that, even without territory, the Islamic State still has vast amounts of information about these people. This is likely to give it even more of an ability to raise revenue as a clandestine terrorist and insurgent group than it possessed prior to 2014. Furthermore, there is evidence that it has hundreds of millions of dollars in reserve, much of that invested in legitimate businesses that will throw off a stream of revenue for years.

Islamic State Expenses

At its peak, operating a state and waging war required the Islamic State to incur substantial costs to pay for salaries for its members, military operations and materiel, the implementation and sustainment of its governing policies, religious policing, its media operations, and its many other varied activities that helped provide it legitimacy. Since the group's inception in the early 2000s, its internal financial documents suggest that it maintained a demanding accounting system to avoid potentially fatal budget deficits and having to seek large amounts of external financing through donations to keep the movement alive.

With the end of the territorial caliphate, there has been a striking decline in Islamic State expenditures, often overlooked by those focusing on what the group is earning. By losing territory, it has reduced its governance costs. By reorganizing as an insurgency, it has reduced its military costs. And by having fewer members and controlling salaries, it has reduced its personnel costs.

Even when the group has been flush with cash, it closely tracked expenses and held its members accountable through an extensive paper trail and oversight at all levels of the organization. When the group was not flush with cash, such as when it was centered in Mosul in 2008 and 2009, it managed to match its salary payments to its revenues, delaying these payments when revenues were low and making up the payments when revenues were higher.

Even with lower revenue and the loss of territory, the Islamic State is still capable of launching complex attacks. This suggests that, even with the loss of the territorial caliphate, as long as it can gain revenue, it will remain a danger.

Policy Options for Preventing Return and Expand

The Islamic State's caliphate was never just territorial. It was always a caliphate of the mind, a vision of an Islamic state that the modern group's leaders imagined to have existed in history and that, were it to exist in reality as its leaders envisioned, would be a regional menace to its neighboring states and a nightmare primarily for the world's Muslims.

If the Islamic State is planning a comeback, which we assess it is, the group will stick with what works—diversifying its financial portfolio to maintain steady and reliable access to financing. What such a reemergence will look like is difficult to project, but its ideology of remaining and expanding, its track record of reemerging from previous defeat, and its actions at maintaining a presence all suggest reemergence is a goal. There are already hints of it, with the group reorganizing its forces in Iraq around Kirkuk and Hawija and north of Mosul, and with the group establishing sleeper cells and conducting attacks in Syria. Although much of the leadership has been killed, and regional and international powers will be much more on guard against an overt territorial presence, the group has been considered defeated before. Its knack for fundraising through criminal activities will prove useful as its members seek to extort, kidnap, kill, steal, smuggle, and traffic to obtain the money they need to survive. Controlling territory would enable these activities, but it is far from a prerequisite. The Islamic State will gain further benefit and freedom of action from the hundreds of millions of dollars it reportedly has in reserve.

Ensuring the demise of the Islamic State will require several intertwined lines of effort: counterterrorism finance, domestic and international intelligence gathering, law enforcement, reconstruction, better government on the part of the Iraq and Syria, and military action. None of these alone will lead to the end of the group. In all cases, the United States and international coalition partners can provide essential support.

The most important measures in Iraq and Syria will be domestic intelligence gathering and law enforcement. Authorities will need to identify businesses that have Islamic State investment, the locations of cash storage sites, and money exchange and transfer businesses that are cooperating with the Islamic State both in Syria and Iraq and throughout the Middle East. Working through law enforcement, authorities will also need to provide security to the population and make sure reconstruction funds are not extorted.

Reconstruction can also help lower the chances of the return of the Islamic State. People have joined the Islamic State and other terrorist groups for a variety of reasons. Although there is a weak link between poverty and adherence to terrorist groups, financial need does cause some people to join. Accordingly, effective stabilization and reconstruction will be important elements in safeguarding Iraq and Syria from the return of the Islamic State.

Ensuring that the Islamic State does not return will also require more inclusive and effective government, especially on the part of the governments of Iraq and Syria. The return of the group from 2009 through 2013 had multiple causes, but perceptions of an unfair and predatory government in Iraq played a significant role.

Although there are still severe problems, including sectarian violence, Iraq appears to be making an effort to improve the way its government operates and treats the country's citizens. Roundups by the Popular Mobilization Units and arrests, raids, and actions at checkpoints by regular Iraqi government forces in areas formerly dominated by the Islamic State could exacerbate existing tensions and lead to renewed grievances among Sunni Arabs who have returned to these areas. Negative perceptions of government have reemerged in some areas. Trends are far more negative in Syria. There, with Russian airpower, the Assad government's military campaign has included extensively bombing civilian areas and using chemical weapons. The government appears to have engaged in a systematic campaign of mass murder and has taken steps to expropriate the property of people who have opposed it or are just refugees or internally displaced.

In both countries, dealing with former and suspected members of the Islamic State will prove a challenge, as will dealing with those who either forcibly or voluntarily cooperated with the group but present no danger. In Iraq, thousands of people are held in detention centers for suspicion of fighting with or otherwise supporting the Islamic State. In

Syria, the Syrian Democratic Forces hold thousands of Islamic State–linked prisoners. A related challenge will be what to do with the many women and children who were associated with the Islamic State, especially children who have known little else or have a poor memory of life before the Islamic State.

Finally, military action will still be required. The war against the Islamic State showed the limits of counterterrorism financing. Sanctions, one of the principal traditional tools for this area of policy, were insufficient to halt the advance of the territorial caliphate, and even the strikes on oil infrastructure and cash storage hurt, but did not stop, the group. Military action will still be needed, at minimum, to capture or kill the many Islamic State cells throughout Iraq and Syria, to guard borders, and to hold territory that may be at risk of recapture.

The United States has a role in all these lines of effort. As long as the Islamic State can act, U.S. partners in the Middle East, allies in Europe, and even the United States itself will be threatened. In considering its policies, the United States must balance two competing issues. The first is that there is little desire for endless military engagement, regardless of the legal foundations for that engagement. The second is that the United States has been crucial to the fight against the Islamic State, and continued engagement will likely be necessary to forestall its return. This engagement need not necessarily feature military action prominently, and U.S. assistance can help across all lines of effort, but a military role will likely be needed. Working with international partners is likely to strengthen U.S. efforts.

The essential role for the United States is to continue its activity regarding Islamic State finances. This has intelligence, military, and training components. The United States and its international partners, even with these partners in the lead, also have a role in law enforcement training and funding. Italy has played a leading role in the law enforcement effort in Iraq.

International involvement is likely to be crucial to stabilization and reconstruction in Iraq and Syria. Such involvement would include, at minimum, financing and assistance with ensuring that reconstruction funds do not leak to the Islamic State and, thus, would also be part of efforts to deny money to the group. Transparency and oversight of funding and financial assistance continuously prove to be a challenge, especially in war zones.

Finally, several aspects of military involvement will remain important. The United States has been a valuable partner in the training and operations of the Iraqi Security Forces, which are likely to need continued assistance. Continued U.S. involvement in these roles not only will help them maintain effectiveness in operations against remnants of the Islamic State but also could forestall degradation and politicization of the Iraqi Security Forces and work to guard against increasing sectarianism, as happened in the years before the Islamic State conquered Mosul.

Syria is entirely different. Even though the United Nations Security Council has unanimously endorsed a Syrian-led, Syrian-owned political transition, there is no sign of such a transition. As of April 2019, the country was essentially divided into zones ruled by different entities. The leading partner of the United States, the Kurdish-dominated Syrian Democratic Forces, is not without problems, especially a link with the Kurdistan Workers Party, a terrorist group fighting an insurgency against America's North Atlantic Treaty Organization ally, Turkey.

However, given the current location of Islamic State elements in Syria and the way the group has maintained its organization and resurged in the past, U.S. involvement with the Syrian Democratic Forces will likely be necessary until a legitimate government takes over Syria, a process that could take years to unfold. In addition, a complete U.S. pullout would likely result in competition among the Syrian Kurds, Turkey, and the Syrian central government and its allies that would give an opening for the Islamic State to strengthen and return. One option would be to strengthen checkpoints and joint patrols between the U.S. and Kurdish forces operating in the area. This could bring a modicum of stability, although such patrols could result in attacks on American troops. Such a role could also be played by a multinational force replacing U.S. forces, but creating such a force has proven difficult, at least as of April 2019.

In a fluid security environment in which there is limited ability or willingness to conduct the type of policing activities that would deter widespread criminality, Islamic State members will once again try to resuscitate a shadow economy in the rural Sunni heartlands. They have a proven track record of doing so successfully. Unlike before 2014, they likely have hundreds of millions of dollars and extensive data on the population, its tribal structure and alliances, and its assets. Just as before 2014, any revival will present a danger that is likely to require the involvement of the United States.

Acknowledgments

The authors thank the Smith Richardson Foundation for sponsoring this research, and particularly for the support of and encouragement from Marin Strmecki, Nadia Schadlow, and Kathy Lavery. Erik Nemeth provided valuable insight into the antiquities trade; Nathan Vest conducted much-needed Arabic translation; Stephan Seabrook provided research support on the economy of Syria; and Benjamin Bahney gave valuable input in early project discussions. Madeline Magnuson and Craig Whiteside provided expert reviews that greatly improved the report. Aside from coauthoring this report, Mona Alami is a nonresident senior fellow at the Atlantic Council. Matthew Byrd guided the manuscript through the RAND publishing process; Phyllis Gilmore provided expert copyediting; and Tanya Maiboroda created the cover art.

Any opinions, findings, conclusions, or recommendations expressed in this publication are those of the authors and do not necessarily reflect the views of any other people or organizations.

CHAPTER ONE

Introduction

When the Islamic State overran the Iraqi city of Mosul in June 2014, one of its most important targets was the city's banks. As it overran Mosul and other cities in northern and western Iraq, the group gained as much as $500 million from bank vaults.[1] Even more startling than the amount gained from banks, however, were revelations that the bank spoils amounted to less than what the group already had in total funds. Only weeks before, Iraqi police captured 160 thumb drives containing hundreds of Islamic State financial records. The documents reportedly showed that the Islamic State had accumulated approximately $875 million in revenue even before the Mosul bank windfall.[2]

The Islamic State used this money to fund its conquest of a territory, which it deemed to be a new caliphate as a successor to the one Islam's founding leaders had established. Centered in Iraq and Syria, this new caliphate at one time was roughly the size of the United Kingdom and had up to 9 million inhabitants. The group paid its members, bought weapons and military supplies, and even paid for services throughout the area it ruled. As it grew, it declared additional prov-

[1] Daniel Glaser, "Remarks by Assistant Secretary for Terrorist Financing Daniel Glaser at Chatham House," Washington, D.C.: U.S. Department of the Treasury, February 8, 2016a. The Islamic State dealt with a variety of currencies, primarily U.S. dollars, Iraqi dinars, and Syrian pounds, as well as gold and other precious metals. In the media and government documents, values are often reported in U.S. dollars, but these values are more appropriately considered to be the dollar-equivalent value in current U.S. dollars.

[2] Martin Chulov, "How an Arrest in Iraq Revealed ISIS's $2bn Jihadist Network," *Guardian*, June 15, 2014.

inces in Egypt, Libya, Algeria, Yemen, Saudi Arabia, and Afghanistan; established affiliated groups in Indonesia, Jordan, Morocco, Turkey, Lebanon, the Philippines, and Nigeria; and placed clandestine operators in still more areas, including Turkey and the Palestinian territories. In Iraq and Syria, the Islamic State controlled oil fields, taxed the inhabitants of its territories, and charged tolls and transit fees, earning hundreds of millions of dollars annually.

As of March 2019, a multinational campaign against the Islamic State had destroyed the territorial caliphate. Led by Iraqi security forces in Iraq and the Syrian Democratic Forces (SDF) in Syria, and supported by the U.S. armed forces, Iraqi Popular Mobilization Units, Iranian forces in Iraq, members of the U.S.-led Combined Joint Task Force–Operation Inherent Resolve (CJTF-OIR), and fighting units from elsewhere, the campaign had isolated the Islamic State as a territorial entity in a small part of the Middle Euphrates River Valley in Syria and, finally, defeated it in its last holdout of Baghouz.[3]

And yet reports of Islamic State activity in many parts of Iraq and Syria continue to emerge. On the battlefront, Iraqi forces came under fire in January 2019 in Ninewa Governorate; in response, they and coalition forces destroyed three tunnels that Islamic State fighters were using as a hideout and to store supplies.[4] Iraqi forces also came under fire in western Anbar Governorate, where the Islamic State remains active.[5] On the financial front, in January 2019, the head of Abi Saida district in Diyala Governorate in Iraq said that the Islamic State controlled most of the villages in the south and that the group was con-

---

[3] CJTF-OIR Public Affairs Office (PAO), "CJTF-OIR Continues Partner Support to Defeat ISIS," press release, December 25, 2018c; CJTF-OIR PAO, "CJTF-OIR, Partner Forces Further Reduce ISIS Influence," press release, January 15, 2019a; Liz Sly and Louisa Loveluck, "The 'Caliphate' Is No More. But the Islamic State Isn't Finished Yet," *Washington Post*, March 23, 2019.

[4] Governorates, sometimes known as provinces, are subnational geographic areas in Iraq and Syria. The Islamic State also designated areas as provinces. We reserve the term *province* for subnational areas declared by the Islamic State and the term *governorate* for the official, nationally designated subnational areas.

[5] CJTF-OIR PAO, "CJTF-OIR, Partner Forces Liberate Additional Syrian Villages," press release, January 19, 2019b.

ducting smuggling operations throughout the governorate as its primary funding mechanism.[6]

Understanding the future of the Islamic State requires an assessment of its finances. In this report, we provide details on the many ways the group has raised money and spent money. We also assess what this financial activity means for the group's likelihood of reemerging. Throughout its history, the Islamic State and its predecessor groups have focused on raising money locally. With this money, the Islamic State has conducted a wide range of terrorist and military operations and even run an actual state, at least for a short time.

A Brief History of the Islamic State

The Islamic State has gone through a variety of iterations (see Table 1.1).[7] Its original core came from a group called Jama'at al-Tawhid wal-Jihad and founded in the 1990s by a Jordanian terrorist and fighter called Abu Musab al-Zarqawi. After training in Afghanistan, Zarqawi went to Iran, Syria, Lebanon, and then eventually Iraq even before the start of the 2003 Iraq war. In the vacuum created by the overthrow of Iraqi leader Saddam Hussein, a variety of insurgent groups became active, including Zarqawi's group.

Zarqawi aligned his group with al-Qa'ida in October 2004, becoming The Organization of the Base of Jihad in Mesopotamia, or al-Qa'ida in Iraq (AQI). Through 2006, the group was strongest in

---

[6] "Director of Abi Saida District: Most of the Villages in the South of the District Are Under the Control of Daesh," Al-Sumaria News (in Arabic), January 23, 2019.

[7] This section draws from Patrick B. Johnston, Jacob N. Shapiro, Howard J. Shatz, Benjamin Bahney, Danielle F. Jung, Patrick K. Ryan, and Jonathan Wallace, *Foundations of the Islamic State: Management, Money, and Terror in Iraq, 2005–2010*, Santa Monica, Calif.: RAND Corporation, RR-1192-DARPA, 2016, and from Howard J. Shatz and Erin-Elizabeth Johnson, *The Islamic State We Knew: Insights Before the Resurgence and Their Implications*, Santa Monica, Calif.: RAND Corporation, RR-1267-OSD, 2015. A valuable account of the group and the roots of the strategy of founding an Islamic state can be found in Brian H. Fishman, *The Master Plan: ISIS, Al-Qaeda, and the Jihadi Strategy for Final Victory*, New Haven, Conn.: Yale University Press, 2016.

Table 1.1
Islamic State Chronology

1990s	Abu Musab al-Zarqawi helps found Jama'at al-Tawhid wal-Jihad, precursor to AQI
2004	Zarqawi joins his group to al-Qa'ida, renaming it The Organization of the Base of Jihad in Mesopotamia, popularly known as AQI
January 2006	AQI forms the Mujahideen Shura Council with other jihadist groups
June 2006	U.S. airstrike kills Zarqawi
October 2006	AQI forms the Islamic State of Iraq (ISI), led by Abu 'Umar al-Baghdadi and Abu Ayyub al-Masri, also known as Abu Hamza al-Muhajir
April 2010	Iraqi and U.S. operation kills Baghdadi and Masri
May 2010	Abu Bakr al-Baghdadi becomes leader
July 2011	Baghdadi sends fighters into Syria; they form the core of what becomes known as Jabhat al-Nusra
April 2013	ISI splits with Nusra; Nusra affiliates with al-Qa'ida and ISI declares itself to be the Islamic State in Iraq and Syria (ISIS)
June 2014	ISIS conquers Mosul, Iraq's second-largest city
June 29, 2014	ISIS declares itself to be the Islamic State
July 2017	The Islamic State is defeated in Mosul, Iraq
October 2017	The Islamic State is defeated in Raqqa, Syria, considered its capital
March 2019	The Islamic State is defeated in Baghouz, Syria, its last overt territorial enclave

Anbar Governorate in western Iraq but had cells and units throughout northern and western Iraq.

In January 2006, AQI organized the formation of an umbrella organization of Sunni jihadist groups called the Mujahideen Shura Council.[8]

[8] As explained further in Chapter Two, AQI and its successors are Salafi-jihadist groups. Salafi characterizes an adherent of an ideological strain in Sunni Islam that seeks to emulate, as purer, the thinking and practices of Muhammad, the leading prophet in Islam, and the earliest generations of Muslims. The term *jihad* can have several connotations, but in the context of violent action, jihadists believe that violent struggle against non-Muslims and Muslims they judge as apostate is an important religious duty.

This was intended as a transitional phase leading up to an Islamic state. A coalition airstrike killed Zarqawi in June 2006, but the group was far from done. Two new leaders eventually took over, known as Abu Ayyub al-Masri, an Egyptian, and Abu 'Umar al-Baghdadi, an Iraqi. In October 2006, eight years before the group stormed into Mosul, al-Masri declared the establishment of the Islamic State of Iraq (ISI) with himself as minister of war and Abu 'Umar al-Baghdadi as emir, or ruler.

The tide began to turn against the group in late 2006, a month before the declaration of ISI, when a group of tribal sheikhs in Anbar Governorate united against AQI. With indigenous opponents and with the United States improving its counterinsurgency strategy, the group, now operating as ISI, was on the defensive from mid-2007. Although it maintained units in much of Iraq, it retained most of its power in Mosul, Iraq's second-largest city, and used the desert area of northwest Iraq and eastern Syria, known as the Jazirah, as a haven. A coalition operation in 2010 killed Abu 'Umar al-Baghdadi and al-Masri, seeming to permanently cripple the group.

ISI, however, proved not only resilient, but regenerative. In fact, in 2011, three analysts long familiar with the group wrote that its track record "suggests that the group's structure and ability to generate local funding and recruits may keep it an effective fighting force long after U.S. troops have left."[9]

After the death of Abu 'Umar al-Baghdadi, a new leader emerged, Abu Bakr al-Baghdadi. He and other leaders set about reconstituting the group, following a strategy of assassinating legitimate authorities, infiltrating localities, and eventually taking control.[10] With the onset of the civil war in Syria, ISI established a new group in that country but declined to claim any affiliation; that group eventually became a separate group, Jabhat al-Nusra, later called Hayat Tahrir al-Sham. In 2013, ISI established an overt presence in Syria, and the leader-

---

9 Benjamin Bahney, Renny McPherson, and Howard J. Shatz, "Glimpse of Bin Laden Techniques in Captured Records of al-Qa'ida in Iraq," Sitrep, GlobalSecurity.org website, May 27, 2011.

10 Craig Whiteside, "War, Interrupted, Part I: The Roots of the Jihadist Resurgence in Iraq," War on the Rocks website, November 5, 2014a, and Craig Whiteside, "War, Interrupted, Part II: From Prisoners to Rulers," War on the Rocks website, November 6, 2014b.

ship renamed the group the Islamic State in Iraq and Syria (ISIS; also known as the Islamic State in Iraq and al-Sham and the Islamic State in Iraq and the Levant [ISIL]).[11] In early 2014, al-Qa'ida disavowed the group, whereupon ISIS became a fully independent entity and a competitor to the older organization. Finally, after the June 2014 conquest of Mosul, ISIS renamed itself the Islamic State, with Abu Bakr al-Baghdadi as its first caliph, the Caliph Ibrahim.

Countering the Islamic State's Finances

Countering the finances of the Islamic State has always been part of the effort to counter the group itself. In August 2014, United Nations Security Council (UNSC) Resolution 2170 called on all United Nations members to take a variety of steps to degrade the Islamic State's financial resources.[12]

In September 2014, the United States announced a strategy to counter the Islamic State, followed by the October 2014 establishment of CJTF-OIR, the U.S. command to lead coalition warfare against the group. One element of the U.S. strategy included finances. Specifically, the strategy deemed "disrupting ISIL's finances" as a core element and noted that the United States was already working with partners in a

> coordinated approach that includes: reducing ISIL's revenue from oil and assets it has plundered; limiting ISIL's ability to extort local populations; stemming ISIL's gains from kidnapping for ransom; and disrupting the flow of external donations to the group. Our domestic laws also provide additional tools in this effort, enabling us to sanction or prosecute those who fund ISIL's activities.[13]

---

[11] The group is sometimes referred to as "of Iraq" rather than "in Iraq," but s, *fi* is used, for which *in* is the best translation.

[12] UNSC, Resolution 2170, August 15, 2014a.

[13] White House, "Fact Sheet: Strategy to Counter the Islamic State of Iraq and the Levant (ISIL)," Washington, D.C.: Office of the Press Secretary, September 10, 2014.

Since then, the United States and its partners have taken a variety of measures to strip the group of its financial resources (Table 1.2). The most important has been taking back territory. As discussed in Chapter Three, the group's revenue-raising capacity has been severely cut back. However, as this report will show, the Islamic State is far from financially destroyed. In fact, it is likely that it has not only enough resources but enough revenue-generating capacity to remain active for years and even to reemerge as a powerful insurgency under the right circumstances.

The Plan for This Report

The report provides information on the Islamic State and its finances with the goal of analyzing whether it might reemerge as a potent insurgency in its core areas of Iraq and Syria. In Chapter Two, we discuss the group's ideology, strategy, and organization. Despite recent debates about ideology, these three elements have remained remarkably constant over time. In Chapter Three, we discuss Islamic State revenue generation. We report how the group raised money as AQI and ISI, how it raised money as the Islamic State with a territorial caliphate, and how it is likely raising money postcaliphate. In Chapter Four, we delve into more detail on revenue, providing on-the-ground evidence of the group's revenue-gathering activities. One notable outcome from these activities was that it was able to gather information on many of the 6 million to 9 million people over whom it ruled when it had a territorial caliphate. In Chapter Five, we discuss Islamic State expenditures. In broad categories, these included compensation for its members, military expenditures, and expenditures for governing. We show that the Islamic State, for all of its existence, was able to maintain tight control of expenditures and match them to revenues. Finally, in Chapter Six, we discuss the Islamic State's current activities; the implications of its financial activity for the likelihood of reemergence; and measures that Iraq, the United States, and their partners can take to counter the Islamic State. These measures are not just financial. Lines of effort to counter the Islamic State are related. Countering finances

Table 1.2
Islamic State Finances Timeline

Date	Event
June 2014	The Islamic State captures Mosul and takes up to $500 million from banks there and elsewhere in Iraq
June and July 2014	The Islamic State captures major Syrian and Iraqi oil and gas fields
Winter–spring 2014–2015	The Central Bank of Iraq ends the ability of about 90 banks in Islamic State territory to make wire transfers
July 2015	The Iraqi government stops payments to employees in Islamic State territory; estimated at $2 billion per year, the Islamic State had been taking a portion for itself
Summer 2015	The United States temporarily cuts off dollar transfers to the Central Bank of Iraq out of concern the Islamic State had access to that U.S. currency
October 2015	Start of Operation Tidal Wave II, the U.S.-led air campaign against the Islamic State's oil assets
December 2015	The Central Bank of Iraq prohibits 142 Islamic State–linked exchange houses from participating in the bank's U.S. dollar auctions
January 2016	First publicly acknowledged strike on an Islamic State cash storage facility under Operation Point Blank
July 2017	Iraqi forces capture Mosul, taking away a major revenue source
October 2017	SDF capture Raqqa, the Islamic State's de facto capital in Syria, taking away a major revenue source
October 2017	SDF capture the al-Omar oil field, Syria's largest

SOURCES: Yaya J. Fanusie and Alex Entz, "Islamic State Financial Assessment," Washington, D.C.: Foundation for Defense of Democracies, Center on Sanctions and Illicit Finance, March 2017; Jennifer Fowler, "Remarks of Deputy Assistant Secretary for Terrorist Financing Jennifer Fowler at the Washington Institute for Near East Policy on U.S. Efforts to Counter the Financing of ISIL," Washington, D.C.: U.S. Department of the Treasury, February 2, 2015; Isabel Coles, "Despair, Hardship as Iraq Cuts Off Wages in Islamic State Cities," Reuters, October 2, 2015; Emily Glazer, Nour Malas, and Jon Hilsenrath, "U.S. Cut Cash to Iraq on Iran, ISIS Fears, Wall Street Journal, November 3, 2015; Glaser, 2016a; Margaret Coker, "How Islamic State's Secret Banking Network Prospers," *Wall Street Journal*, February 24, 2016; Cheryl Pellerin, "Inherent Resolve Spokesman: Coalition Operations Deny ISIL's Caliphate Dreams," DoD News website, May 13, 2016; Louisa Loveluck and Mustafa Salim, "Iraq's Prime Minister Announces Victory Against the Islamic State in Mosul," *Washington Post*, July 10, 2017; Anne Barnard and Hwaida Saad, "Raqqa, ISIS 'Capital,' Is Captured, U.S.-Backed Forces Say," *New York Times*, October 17, 2017; and Ellen Francis, "U.S. Backed Militias Seize Key Oil Field in East Syria: SDF," Reuters, October 22, 2017.

alone will not stop the group, just as a military campaign alone will not stop the group. The Islamic State appears intent on reemerging, but the probability of that can be lowered with strong law enforcement efforts; continued U.S. military involvement through training, air support, and generally working with local partners on the ground; and inclusive government on the part of Iraq and whatever system takes hold in Syria. Although it is impossible to predict whether the three factors of strong law enforcement, continued U.S. military partnering, and inclusive government will move in positive directions, we suggest there is a large risk that they will not.

CHAPTER TWO

The Islamic State's Ideology, Strategy, and Organization

The Islamic State's ideology, strategy, and organizational structure all contribute to its culture and operational and tactical behavior, which in turn directly affect and are supported by its financial behavior and economic decisionmaking. Although much of the focus on the Islamic State tends to analyze how the group interacts with the outside world, what is often overlooked is that the Islamic State has consistently sought to reshape its identity among Sunnis.[1] Moreover, substantial infighting accompanied the collapse of the caliphate toward the end of 2017.

Historical Overview

As an organization, the Islamic State has been significantly influenced by the worldview and doctrine of its founding leader, Abu Musab al-Zarqawi. Zarqawi, a Jordanian who was radicalized in prison—in particular, by the influence of leading jihadi scholar Abu Muhammad al-Maqdisi.[2] Zarqawi viewed non-Sunni Muslim civilians as legitimate targets of violence and made such violence a centerpiece of the organization's strategy. His philosophy and actions remain fundamen-

---

[1] Craig Whiteside, "Nine Bullets for the Traitors, One for the Enemy: The Slogans and Strategy behind the Islamic State's Campaign to Defeat the Sunni Awakening (2006–2017)," The Hague: International Centre for Counter-Terrorism, September 2018.

[2] Joby Warrick, *Black Flags: The Rise of ISIS*, New York: Anchor, 2015; Joas Wagemakers, "Invoking Zarqawi: Abu Muhammad al-Maqdisi's Jihad Deficit," *CTC Sentinel*, Vol. 2, No. 6, June 2009.

tal to the present-day Islamic State's ideology and strategy.[3] But it is important to note that Zarqawi did not value sectarian conflict as an end in itself but rather as the means to an end. This means dovetailed with his broader strategy of creating a caliphate, something the newly empowered Shia of Iraq would most certainly fight to oppose.[4]

Zarqawi's approach to jihad marks an important difference between the Islamic State and al-Qa'ida in terms of the targets of their violence. This difference strained relations between the two groups when the Islamic State was officially an al-Qa'ida affiliate starting in 2004 and has contributed to divides between the Islamic State and Jabhat al-Nusra [the Nusra Front], an al-Qa'ida–linked group in Syria. Originally founded as the Syrian branch of the Islamic State predecessor organization ISI, Nusra's differences with its parent group became particularly visible when ISI moved overtly into Syria and declared itself as the Islamic State in Iraq and Syria in 2013. Nusra splintered from the Islamic State and reaffirmed its allegiance to al-Qa'ida and that organization's leader, Ayman al-Zawahiri.[5]

---

3 New scholarship, translations, and document discoveries continue to fill in information on the origins of the Islamic State, information that is necessarily incomplete because of the group's clandestine nature. There is evidence that the group's extremist views, including justification for killing Shia and other Muslims, stemmed from a leading member named Abdulrahman al-Qaduli, also known as Abu Ali al-Anbari, who developed them throughout the 1990s and early 2000s (Hassan Hassan, "The True Origins of ISIS," *Atlantic*, November 30, 2018e).

4 There is also a practical, strategic reason for fostering such sectarian hatred: It would have been impossible for the group to establish a caliphate in a Shia state (we thank a knowledgeable reader for this observation).

5 In July 2016, Nusra officially announced that it had split from al-Qa'ida and renamed itself Jabhat Fateh al-Sham [the Front for the Conquest of the Levant]. Experts believe that Jabhat Fateh al-Sham remained aligned with al-Qa'ida but officially split from it to rebrand itself as a predominantly Syrian group. See Aymenn Jawad Al-Tamimi, "Al-Qa'ida Uncoupling: Jabhat Al-Nusra's Rebranding as Jabhat Fateh Al-Sham," *CTC Sentinel*, Vol. 9, No. 8, August 22, 2016c. Nusra later formed Hayat Tahrir al-Sham [Assembly for the Liberation of the Levant] with Harakat Nur al Din al Zinki, Liwa al Haqq, Ansar al Din, and Jaysh al Sunna, plus other groups. However, in July 2017, clashes within the group essentially led to it being largely, if not exclusively, Nusra (Counter Extremism Project, *Nusra Front [Jabhat Fateh al-Sham]*, New York, 2018).

Ideology and Ideological Rifts

The Islamic State subscribes to an extreme variant of Salafi-jihadist ideology that emphasizes adherence to monotheistic Islamist governance and is highly sectarian. Salafism is strictly Sunni.[6] Salafists define Islam as anything that was explicitly practiced by Muhammad, the prophet of Islam, and that was upheld by the first three generations of his Sunni followers (until the ninth century).[7] Salafism is differentiated from generic "Islamism" by the fact that Salafism is defined as nonpolitical. Salafis believe not just in the spirit but in the letter of the law, setting them apart from their mainstream counterparts.[8] The Islamic State's Salafist ideology draws from Wahhabism, a particularly austere strain of Salafism found largely in Saudi Arabia.[9] Salafi groups have sought to purify Islam of what they view as centuries of deviance from true Islam, including Shiism, Sufism, and non-Salafist Sunnism.[10]

Jihadism has multiple interpretations. At its most peaceful, it can be interpreted as a personal struggle against one's evil inclinations or as a struggle to improve the morality of the Islamic community.[11] Within the context of Salafi-jihadism, it involves the idea that Muslims have an obligation to engage in religiously sanctioned warfare and that all able-

---

[6] Sunni Islam is one of two major branches of Islam, with Shia Islam the other. The two differ on their views of the rightful succession of the leadership of Islam. Shia Muslims believe succession flows through Muhammad's son-in-law, Ali ibn Abi Talib, and his sons. Sunni Muslims believe succession ran through the first four leaders, the so-called rightly guided caliphs, of which Ali was one, but not Ali's descendants. Sufis, another type of Muslim, are Islamic mystics and may be either Sunni or Shia. See "Shii Islam," "Sunni Islam," and "Sufism" in John L. Esposito, ed., *The Oxford Dictionary of Islam*, Oxford: Oxford University Press, 2003 (online edition).

[7] Jacob Olidort, "What Is Salafism? How a Nonpolitical Ideology Became a Political Force," *Foreign Affairs*, November 24, 2015.

[8] Shadi Hamid and Rashid Dar, "Islamism, Salafism, and Jihadism: A Primer," Markaz blog, Washington, D.C.: Brookings Institution, July 15, 2016.

[9] Hassan Hassan, "The Sectarianism of the Islamic State: Ideological Roots and Political Context," Washington, D.C.: Carnegie Endowment for International Peace, June 13, 2016a.

[10] Olidort, 2015.

[11] "Jihad," in Esposito, 2003.

bodied Muslims should take up the mantle of jihad.[12] Salafi-jihadism is a specific approach to jihadism that combines the notions of jihadism with those of Salafism. Given their belief that Salafi-jihadism is the only authentic form of Islam, the Islamic State and other Salafi-jihadist groups justify violence against non-Salafists based on *takfir*, or the excommunication of fellow Muslims. The Islamic State thus views violence against these "apostates" as legitimate.[13] The Islamic State has taken *takfirism* (the practice of declaring other Muslims to be nonbelievers due to their supposed apostasy or heresy) to new extremes.[14] It has used these ideas opportunistically to exploit extant sectarian divides throughout the Islamic world. The Islamic State's ideological extremism, and the branding it has used to rationalize its actions, helped it surpass al-Qa'ida as the most attractive destination for potential jihadist recruits, at least during its period of rapid growth and peak power, 2013 to 2016.[15] Although the Islamic State's takfiri ideas and actions emerged in part from al-Qa'ida, the group's ideological rigidity separates the two groups. As the analyst Hassan Hassan puts it, "[The Islamic State's] refusal to bend creates a culture of takfirism within takfirism."[16] There has also been a heated debate within jihadist circles about the concept of *hukm al-tatarrus* (the killing of innocent Muslims as a result of terrorist or military operations). As with other acts of violence, the Islamic State takes a more expansive view, justifying such deaths, whereas al-Qa'ida has become gradually more restrictive.[17]

---

[12] Dar and Hamid, 2016.

[13] Dar and Hamid, 2016.

[14] Hassan, 2016a.

[15] The Islamic State was also successful at recruiting in the United States. See Heather J. Williams, Nathan Chandler, and Eric Robinson, *Trends in the Draw of Americans to Foreign Terrorist Organizations from 9/11 to Today*, Santa Monica, Calif.: RAND Corporation, RR-2545-OSD, 2018.

[16] Hassan, 2016a.

[17] Daniel Byman, "Divisions Within the Global Jihad: A Primer," *Lawfare*, September 29, 2017; see also Jack Barclay, "Al-Tatarrus: al-Qaeda's Justification for Killing Muslim Civilians," *Jamestown Terrorism Monitor*, Vol. 8, No. 34, September 9, 2010.

The subject that has led to the most vigorous debate has been over who can claim to be a proper, devout, and righteous Muslim. Ultimately, the Islamic State's leadership recognized that its strict takfiri practices might be counterproductive, especially as the group was losing territory and needed to rejuvenate its ranks with an influx of new recruits. In September 2017, Islamic State religious leadership appeared to soften its stance on this matter, issuing a revocation of an earlier religious edict that broadened the scope of takfirism.[18] Still, the debate continued to rage, with the ideological rift mostly centered on whether those who remain reticent to excommunicate apostates and unbelievers should themselves be excommunicated.[19]

Strategy and State-Building

The Islamic State differentiates itself from groups such as al-Qaʿida by virtue of its strategy. Simply put, the Islamic State seeks to build an actual territorial Islamic state in the form of a caliphate. Although the Islamic State rose to prominence during its brazen offensive in Iraq in June 2014, the group had begun to lay the groundwork for an Islamic state in Iraq almost a decade before. The control of territory was a deliberate decision the Islamic State made and a source of continuity from its earliest days, harkening back to its formative period in the mid-2000s, when it was AQI. Even though controlling territory outright makes the group vulnerable in some important ways, namely to coalition airpower, the group has gone to great lengths to mitigate this by minimizing the exposure of its key leaders when possible. On balance, the group's actions are consistent with a decision that the risks are ultimately worth taking in exchange for controlling more territory and the populations and resources within that territory.[20] The Islamic

---

[18] Thomas Joscelyn, "Islamic State Rescinds One of Its Most Problematic Religious Rulings," *Long War Journal*, September 20, 2017.

[19] Cole Bunzel, "A House Divided: Origins and Persistence of the Islamic State's Ideological Divide," *Jihadica*, June 5, 2018a.

[20] For more on how the Islamic State views control of territory, see Burak Kadercan, "Territorial Logic of the Islamic State: An Interdisciplinary Approach," *Territory, Politics, Gover-*

State has long attempted to manage urban populations: al-Qaim and Fallujah (2004), Mosul (2005), Ramadi (2006), and numerous Syrian and Iraqi cities starting in 2013 and 2014. A significant part of this strategy was that territory could be expanded over time and linked together in service of the eventual establishment of an Islamic state.[21] There are both ideological reasons behind the drive to control territory and more-practical reasons associated with propaganda, recruitment, and the control of vital resources to fund the organization.

Declaration of the State

Starting in early 2006, AQI began to evolve rapidly toward what culminated in its initial declaration of the Islamic State. First, it attracted support from other insurgent movements in Iraq, which resulted in a merger between AQI and five other groups in January 2006 under the banner of a group called the Mujahideen Shura Council, and then ISI, which was officially declared in October 2006 and which the group considers the birth of the Islamic State.[22] Indeed, ISI published its own declaration of statehood, a 115-page manifesto entitled "Informing the People About the Birth of the Islamic State of Iraq."[23] Not only that, but it designated a *commander of the faithful*, a term historically reserved for Islamic caliphs.[24]

ISI moved to establish its bona fides as a state by announcing a cabinet structure and the (pseudonymous) names of the cabinet

---

nance, Vol. 7, No. 1, March 2019.

[21] Joby Warrick, Will McCants, and Aaron Y. Zelin, "The Rise of ISIS: 'Remaining and Expanding,'" Washington Institute for Near East Policy, PolicyWatch 2522, November 12, 2015.

[22] In addition to AQI, the other groups making up the Mujahideen Shura Council included Jaysh al-Ta 'ifa al-Mansura, Saraya 'Ansar al-Tawhid, Saraya al-Jihad al-Islami, Saraya al-Ghuraba, and Kataib al-Ahwal. See, for example, Charles Lister, "Profiling the Islamic State," Doha: Brookings Doha Center, Analysis Paper 13, November 2014, p. 8.

[23] Furqan Establishment for Media Production, "Informing the People About the Birth of the Islamic State of Iraq: A Research on the Establishment of the Islamic State of Iraq, the Motives for Its Establishment, Its Connection to the Future of the Jihadist March, and Its Important Political Roles," 2006.

[24] Whiteside, 2018.

officials who would administer the state's various bureaucracies. ISI's announcement of its first cabinet included ministries of War, Sharia Affairs, Public Relations, Security, Information, Martyrs and Prisoners Affairs, Oil, Agriculture and Fisheries, and Health.[25] The hierarchical, bureaucratic institutions ISI established mirrored al-Qa'ida's blueprint for a jihadi organization, but with the key difference that ISI's focus on seizing, holding, and administering territory made it more akin to a nation-state than was al-Qa'ida, which focused more on training operatives to conduct guerrilla warfare and terrorist attacks outside Afghanistan.[26]

The declaration of an Islamic State in Iraq caused controversy within the jihadi world. Above all, it was unclear whether there was any de facto basis for the declaration of a state. By late 2006 and especially from 2007 onward, the group held little territory, particularly compared with AQI when the Zarqawi-led incarnation of the group was at its zenith in 2004 and 2005. Critics argued that it was irresponsible to declare an Islamic State without first satisfying the basic preconditions for statehood, such as being able to hold territory and govern Sunni populations. Second, some Islamic scholars called into question the legitimacy of the ISI emir (or leader) Abu 'Umar al-Baghdadi, whom the group referred to as the commander of the faithful. In fact, the U.S. military initially believed that Baghdadi was a fictitious Iraqi character—suggested by the pseudonym *al-Baghdadi*—invented by AQI to provide increased legitimacy to the group's Iraqi members, whose commitment to Zarqawi's presumed successor, the Egyptian jihadist Abu Ayyub al-Masri (also known as Abu Hamza al-Muhajir), was uncertain.[27] As discussed later, Abu 'Umar al-Baghdadi turned out to be very real.

[25] SITE Institute, "Islamic State of Iraq Announces Establishment of the Cabinet of its First Islamic Administration in Video Issued Through al-Furqan Foundation," April 19, 2007.

[26] Johnston et al., 2016.

[27] Joel Wing, "Who Was Al Qaeda in Iraq's Abu Omar al-Baghdadi? Interview with Naval War College's Prof. Craig Whiteside," Musings on Iraq website, June 13, 2016.

"Remaining and Expanding"

Up against the difficulties resulting from the tribal revolts in Iraq that started in mid-2006 (known as the Sunni Awakening), the 2007 U.S. troop surge, and a relentless counterterrorism campaign that targeted ISI leadership, ISI struggled to disabuse critics of the notion that the group was, if anything, a failed state. It became a shell of its former self, having lost significant territory, influence, and revenue in its previous strongholds in Anbar Governorate and the greater Baghdad area, including Baghdad's suburbs, or "belts." Despite ISI's waning battlefield and governance capabilities, documents captured from the group in 2009 and 2010 show that it sought to maintain a bureaucratic blueprint similar to the one it had cultivated since the group's early days as AQI in Anbar Governorate.

Even with that intention, the group was unable to build statelike institutions at scale after its initial declaration of an Islamic State in Iraq, according to documents captured in a Special Forces raid against ISI number three, Abu Qaswarah, in 2008. ISI had detailed plans for partitioning the Sunni areas of the country into sectors (roughly akin to Iraq's district level, the country's second-level administrative unit, below the governorate or province level), renaming them based on Quranic traditions, and staffing them with qualified ISI operatives, but the group's capacity was limited. One record from the document cache, which contains sector-level data on ISI's staffing of overall emirs, sharia emirs, military emirs, and media emirs for 30 sectors, reveals that ISI filled only 38 percent of these positions as of the document's production date. Twelve of the 30 sectors (40 percent) lacked an overall emir; 19 (63 percent) lacked a sharia emir; 13 (43 percent) lacked a military emir; and, strikingly, none of the sector-level media emir positions were reported as occupied—a stark contrast to the Islamic State's prolific media bureaucracy as it existed at the peak of the group's strength in 2014 and 2015.[28] Moreover, multinational and Iraqi forces dealt what many believed was a death blow to ISI in April 2010 when a raid on a

---

28 Johnston et al., 2016, pp. 96–100.

safe house near Tikrit killed the group's top two leaders, Abu 'Umar al-Baghdadi and Abu Ayyub al-Masri.[29]

Still, ISI withstood the losses of the two leaders and elevated a new leader—Abu Bakr al-Baghdadi—as the group's new emir and commander of the faithful.[30] And even with the severe losses it suffered after 2007, ISI was able to conduct operations against its enemies throughout Iraq. In 2008 and 2009, its then-leader, Abu 'Umar al-Baghdadi, had announced campaigns to eliminate the Sunni Awakening members who had fought against it, Shia militias, and government officials and political candidates. These operations were carried out by small cells with otherwise little direct guidance. They accounted for thousands of deaths through 2013, helping bring about the reemergence of the group.[31]

Just a few months after the Islamic State declared the establishment—or redeclared the establishment, given the 2006 declaration—of the Islamic State caliphate, the group's English-language magazine featured an article called "Remaining and Expanding" on its cover and had a long story about how it would do just that.[32] The article tied the idea of remaining directly to a speech given by Abu 'Umar al-Baghdadi in April 2007, in which he said, "and indeed, the Islamic State will remain."[33] The theme appeared elsewhere in the magazine, with one article concluding:

> Let the forces of kufr [disbelief, essentially those who do not believe in Islam] do what they can to wage war against it, for the

[29] Tim Arango, "Top Qaeda Leaders in Iraq Reported Killed in Raid," *New York Times*, April 19, 2010.

[30] Cole Bunzel, "From Paper State to Caliphate: The Ideology of the Islamic State," Washington, D.C.: Brookings Institution, The Brookings Project on U.S. Relations with the Islamic World Analysis Paper No. 19, March 2015. See discussion on pp. 25–34.

[31] Craig Whiteside, "The Islamic State and the Return of Revolutionary Warfare," *Small Wars & Insurgencies*, Vol. 27, No. 5, August 2016a.

[32] "Remaining and Expanding," *Dabiq*, No. 5, Muharram 1436 [October–November 2014].

[33] Quoted in "Remaining and Expanding," 2014, p. 32.

> Islamic State, by Allah's permission, will only continue to move forward. Remaining and expanding . . . .[34]

The Importance of the Role of Territory

The effort to remain and expand is emblematic of the role of territory in the group's ideology and strategy. The caliphate was not the Islamic State's first attempt at territorial control. As noted earlier, it took over cities and managed urban populations even in its early days as AQI. Even as it was being pushed back in the late 2000s, it embarked on a deliberate strategy to reemerge and retake territory. After 2010, the increasing marginalization of Iraqi Sunnis helped clear the way for what was then ISI to reassert control in the Sunni-dominated areas where it once held sway.[35]

One consistent thread running throughout the evolution of the Islamic State's tactics has been its commitment to using discriminate violence as a means of taking over new territory and eliminating any rivals.[36] The group underwent an organizational restructuring, implementing functional bureaus that would allow it to exert control over territory more efficiently. It was around the time of the U.S. withdrawal from Iraq at the end of 2011 that the group's leadership began planning for what would come next, specifically, the creation of support zones and lines of effort focused on logistics, two innovations that would contribute to the seeming relative ease with which it captured and controlled large swaths of territory once it began its offensive in earnest over the next few years.[37] By 2013, it was apparent that the Islamic State was once again holding territory, following a hiatus of six years in which the group struggled to do so more broadly.[38] Even

---

[34] "Unifying the Ranks," *Dabiq*, No. 5, Muharram 1436 [October–November 2014], p. 13.

[35] Whiteside, 2014a.

[36] Craig Whiteside, "ISIL's Small Ball Warfare: An Effective Way to Get Back Into the Game," War on the Rocks website, April 29, 2015.

[37] Craig Whiteside, "New Masters of Revolutionary Warfare: The Islamic State Movement (2002–2016)," *Perspectives on Terrorism*, Vol. 10, No. 4, August 2016b, p. 15.

[38] Whiteside, 2016a, p. 763.

its branches abroad (not the focus of this report) have territorial goals. In May 2017, an Islamic State–affiliated group in the Philippines captured the city of Marawi using tactics employed by the Islamic State in Iraq.[39] The Armed Forces of the Philippines finally expelled the group in October 2017, five months after the conquest.[40]

Capturing and holding territory has been a major element of the group's strategy, but depending on other contextual factors, the group was more or less successful in achieving this. Certainly, the U.S. withdrawal, coupled with the chaos brought about as a result of the Syrian civil war, dramatically expanded the Islamic State's opportunity to seize territory, hold it, and eventually begin building its state. This happened concurrently with an influx of tens of thousands of foreign fighters into Iraq and Syria.[41] And while the Islamic State was opportunistic in the territory it conquered, it was also strategic. By focusing on large population centers and major cities, including Mosul, the group was able to scale up its state-building project and then extort and tax the population living in this area, expanding its coffers in the process. "Militants monetized every inch of the territory they conquered, taxing every bushel of wheat, every liter of sheep's milk and every watermelon sold at markets they controlled," according to a report by Rukmini Callimachi, based on original documents.[42] The Islamic State also focused on controlling territory that could serve as logistical hubs, including border crossings along the Syria-Iraq border and such areas as Deir Ezzor, which provided the group access to such critical resources as oil.

---

[39] Lead Inspector General for Overseas Contingency Operations, *Operation Inherent Resolve: Report to the United States Congress, July 1, 2017–September 30, 2017*, Washington, D.C., November 3, 2017b.

[40] Lead Inspector General for Overseas Contingency Operations, *Operation Inherent Resolve and Operation Pacific Eagle—Philippines: Report to the United States Congress, October 1, 2017–December 31, 2017*, Washington, D.C., February 2, 2018.

[41] Edwin Bakker and Mark Singleton, "Foreign Fighters in the Syria and Iraq Conflict: Statistics and Characteristics of a Rapidly Growing Phenomenon," in Andrea de Guttry, Francesca Capone, and Christophe Paulussen, eds., *Foreign Fighters Under International Law and Beyond*, The Hague: T.M.C. Asser Press, 2016, pp. 9–25.

[42] Rukmini Callimachi, "The ISIS Files," *New York Times*, April 4, 2018.

Control of territory not only provided resources to the group and helped it expand its power but also enabled it to amplify its destruction. The Islamic State's control of territory was devastating for several reasons. First, there was the plight of civilians living in these areas. Military-age males were forced to join the group or face punishment. Women were treated harshly and, in the case of minority groups, such as the Yazidis, they were forced into sexual slavery, one of the most egregious violations of human rights that has occurred since World War II.[43] Second, by controlling territory, the Islamic State had the chance to declare a caliphate and, in the process, make joining its ranks even more attractive to legions of followers from around the world. Because the group has held territory, there is also now the promise of future glory once the territory is ultimately reclaimed. Referring to the importance of territory and especially the caliphate, Haroro Ingram and Craig Whiteside have observed, "if it happened before it can happen again."[44] Finally, the control of territory goes beyond the declaration of a caliphate and is directly linked to the importance of a safe haven. Uncontested control of territory helps enable the plotting of external attacks and accumulation of resources that expand a terrorist or insurgent group's ability to achieve its objectives.

A lingering question is not whether territory is integral to the success of the Islamic State—it is.[45] Rather, there is a more pressing question in the immediate term: Just how little territory does the Islamic State need to control to sustain a low-level clandestine terrorist campaign that will allow it to bide time and slowly rebuild its organization? The Islamic State still possesses more than enough money to survive as an organization and thrive once again, owing to potential missteps by the Iraqi and Syrian governments and the militants' ability to persuade

43 Rukmini Callimachi, "ISIS Enshrines a Theology of Rape," *New York Times*, August 13, 2015.

44 Haroro J. Ingram and Craig Whiteside, "The Caliph's Role in the (un)Surprising Resilience of the Islamic State," Foreign Policy Research Institute website, October 25, 2018; see also Colin P. Clarke and Haroro J. Ingram, "After the Caliphate Project: Defeating the ISIS Nostalgia Narrative," Foreign Policy Research Institute website, April 18, 2018.

45 "Does ISIS Need Territory to Survive?" *New York Times*, October 21, 2016.

Sunni Arabs in both countries that the group is the most legitimate entity on the ground, especially at the local level.[46]

Financial Strategy and Doctrine

Since its inception under founding leader Abu Musab al-Zarqawi, the Islamic State has held a consistent financial strategy that aims to support and advance the group's broader religious and state-building goals. The Islamic State's financial strategy and doctrine are characterized by three facets:

- The group strives to be self-sufficient financially.
- It derives its basic rules and governance of the economy from Islamic economic principles.
- Despite these principles, the Islamic State maintains the capacity for significant adaptability and resilience to changing circumstances, battlefield environments, and economic shocks, sometimes deviating from its basic principles to ensure its survival as an organization and its ability to wage jihad in service to its state-building goals.

We discuss the first two of these tenets below and reserve our discussion of the third tenet for subsequent chapters, when we review the Islamic State's revenues and expenditures.

Perhaps the most important characteristic of the Islamic State's financial strategy—and the most vexing for counter–terrorist financing efforts—is its emphasis on financial self-sufficiency.[47] This empha-

---

[46] For more on the future of Islamic State financing, see David Kenner, "All ISIS Has Left Is Money. Lots of It," *Atlantic*, March 24, 2019; see also Joby Warrick, "Retreating ISIS Army Smuggled a Fortune in Cash and Gold Out of Iraq and Syria," *Washington Post*, December 21, 2018.

[47] Benjamin Bahney, Howard J. Shatz, Carroll Ganier, Renny McPherson, Barbara Sude, Sara Beth Elson, and Ghassan Schbley, *An Economic Analysis of the Financial Records of al-Qa'ida in Iraq*, Santa Monica, Calif.: RAND Corporation, MG-1026-OSD, 2010; David S. Cohen, "The Islamic State and Terrorist Financing," written testimony for House Financial Services Committee, November 13, 2014b, p. 3; Patrick B. Johnston, "Countering

sis on financial self-sufficiency was a conscious decision made early in the group's history.[48] Through its various iterations, the Islamic State has funded itself almost entirely from capital and labor from within the territory and populations over which it has direct or indirect control or influence in Iraq and Syria.[49] Unlike other groups, the Islamic State derives a relatively small proportion of its funding from donations and charities outside Iraq and Syria.[50] Consequently, the Islamic State's financing within Iraq and Syria has not depended on moving money through the formal international financial system or maintaining strong ties to outsiders to whom it would be beholden for financing.[51] The Islamic State's self-sufficiency is one of the main reasons that analysts believe the group will continue to earn revenue even without having access to large swaths of territory.[52]

ISIL's Financing," testimony presented before the House Financial Services Committee on November 13, 2014, Santa Monica, Calif.: RAND Corporation, CT-419, 2014; Shatz and Johnson, 2015; and Johnston et al., 2016.

48 "Analysis of the State of ISI" (English trans.), Combating Terrorism Center at West Point Harmony Program website, NMEC-2007-612449, undated. This was reiterated in a subsequent document dating from 2013–2014, Abu Abdullah al-Masri, "Principles in the Administration of the Islamic State," Ch. 6, trans. Aymenn Jawad Al-Tamimi, in "The Isis Papers: A Masterplan for Consolidating Power," *Guardian*, December 7, 2015.

49 John F. Burns and Kirk Semple, "U.S. Finds Insurgency Has Funds to Sustain Itself," *New York Times*, November 26, 2006; Bahney, Shatz, et al., 2010, pp. 14–15; and Johnston et al., 2016, pp. 205–206.

50 Of particular note, Qatar is alleged to have played a role in Jabhat al Nusra's decision in July 2016 to rename itself Jabhat Fateh al-Sham and claim that it had broken ties with all foreign parties, namely al-Qa'ida. According to sources cited in a Reuters investigation, intelligence officials from Qatar and other Gulf states met several times with Nusra's leader starting in 2015 to attempt to bolster the group by providing money, arms, and materiel, conditional on it breaking away from al-Qa'ida. See Mariam Karouny, "Insight—Syria's Nusra Front May Leave Qaeda to Form New Entity," Reuters, March 4, 2015; Tom Finn, "Qatar's Channel to Militants Possibly Dangerous, Possibly Useful," Reuters, December 18, 2015. Quoted in David Andrew Weinberg, *Qatar and Terror Finance Part II: Private Funders of al-Qaeda in Syria*, Washington, D.C.: Foundation for Defense of Democracies, January 2017, p. 6.

51 Cohen, 2014b, p. 3.

52 Colin P. Clarke, "ISIS's New Plans to Get Rich and Wreak Havoc," *Foreign Policy*, October 10, 2018.

The second tenet of the Islamic State's financial strategy is that it is rooted in principles of Islamic economics, as interpreted by Salafi-jihadist economists and religious scholars. Islamic economics has been defined as

> the knowledge and application of injunctions and rules of the Shari'ah that prevent injustice in the acquisition and disposal of material resources in order to provide satisfaction to human beings and enable them to perform their obligations to Allah and the society.[53]

Many primary-source Islamic State financial documents, including both captured documents and documents disseminated by the Islamic State, paint a clear picture of the principles intended to govern the Islamic State's economy and financing.[54] Scholars note that Islam has an affinity for capitalism: It permits private property and private ownership of the means of production, supports free enterprise, and holds trade and production in high esteem.[55] This view can be seen in the doctrine the Islamic State applied to running the economy of its caliphate.

Administering Wealth

Just as the Islamic State was about to seize large swaths of territory in Syria and Iraq, the group laid out several pillars of its strategy for "the administration of wealth." In "Principles in the Administration of the Islamic State," dated Islamic year 1435, or western year November 2013 to September 2014, and written under the name Abu Abdullah al-Masri, the Islamic State devoted an entire chapter to guidance on "Administration of the Projects." This involved basic financial doctrine on how it would regulate the economy and intervene directly in certain industries to monopolize control over these economic sectors.

---

[53] S. M. Hasanuz Zaman, "Definition of Islamic Economics," *Journal of Research in Islamic Economics*, Vol. 1, No. 2, 1984, pp. 49–50.

[54] al-Masri, 2015, Ch. 7.

[55] Zubair Hasan, "Theory of Profit: The Islamic Viewpoint," *Journal of Research in Islamic Economics*, Vol. 1, No. 1, 1983, pp. 3–14.

The Islamic State prohibited non–Islamic State ownership of what it viewed as strategic resources, including oil, gold, and antiquities.[56] The Islamic State collected sales revenue directly from these industries. On oil, the group stated that

> it is not allowed for a person who has no pledge of allegiance on his neck to the caliph to invest in an oil or gas field or what has arisen from their trajectory, but it is allowed besides that to produce derivatives after buying the crude products from the fields of the Islamic State, just as it is allowed to sell and deal in them inside and outside the state.[57]

On gold and antiquities—treasures from the ground, as the group categorized them—there were special rules. The group decreed that "it is not allowed to excavate for gold and antiquities except by expressed agreement from the resources department, and all transferred and stored materials will be confiscated for the interest of the treasury."[58] However, dealing in gold that was not excavated from the ground—gold that was already in circulation, presumably including the gold dinar currency the Islamic State sought to circulate as its official currency—was not prohibited.[59]

For private enterprise and investors, the Islamic State sought to protect property rights by providing protection based on agreements and contracts approved by the Islamic State, which could impose

---

[56] The Islamic State also prohibited investment in weapons and, indeed, exerted strict gun control regulations in areas under its control. According to the Islamic State's "Principles in the Administration of the Islamic State" document, the Islamic State's doctrine stated that

> it is forbidden to establish factories to produce weapons and materials particular to them without granting of any explicit permits for the situation, just as it is forbidden to establish shops to sell public weapons besides personal weapons and deal in them without prior knowledge and agreement from the responsible military emir in the wilayat [province or governorate].

See al-Masri, 2015, Ch. 7.

[57] al-Masri, 2015, Ch. 7.

[58] al-Masri, 2015, Ch. 7.

[59] al-Masri, 2015, Ch. 7.

regulations on production, exports, and prices to advance the state's interests. The Islamic State's at-times muscular interference in markets would generally be viewed as dubious economic policy, but, compared to the weak institutions and corruption of the more-legitimate governments that preceded Islamic State rule in Iraq and Syria, the group's ability to impose a rule-based order might have actually stabilized markets and increased economic activity in some places.[60]

In certain respects, many of the Islamic State's basic economic principles are similar to the market-based reforms and institutional capacity-building policies commonly prescribed by international financial institutions. Moreover, the group's views on investment are fairly sophisticated in their consideration of productivity and risk avoidance:

> The independence of the investor from the administration of the province is a more preferred means for the administration of the wealth, increasing local production and improving the capability of the producing material, and regulating the time and expenditure. And it will [also] be a better guarantee against losses resulting from any sizeable investment project.
>
> For the independent foundation is outside the limits of liability that arise for those projects that are affiliated with a province of the Islamic State.
>
> And it is not right for the investor according to the law, to hand over the production to those who have no right to it and they [those who have the right to it] are the ones determined in an agreement by the administration that is entrusted over the project and overseeing its organization by the province in which the project is established.
>
> And such an agreement is stipulated on determining the beneficiaries and the means of profit with the guarantee of the [Islamic]

---

[60] For an analysis of the economy under the Islamic State, see Eric Robinson, Daniel Egel, Patrick B. Johnston, Sean Mann, Alexander D. Rothenberg, and David Stebbins, *When the Islamic State Comes to Town: The Economic Impact of Islamic State Governance in Iraq and Syria*, Santa Monica, Calif.: RAND Corporation, RR-1970-RC, 2017.

> State to convey the products internally to the borders of the Islamic State without exposing them to any risk.[61]

Moreover, the Islamic State's economic strategy called for at least a modicum of administrative capability and technical expertise because, "for the other principal goods that also come under the crux of people's lives, the officials must know about all means of operation and production like dealing in water, flour and livestock."[62]

Conclusion

As the Islamic State faced defeat on the battlefield it began to look like less of a monolith as organizational disputes arose over ideology. The debate, which centered on takfirism, hukm al-tatarrus, sharia law, and when to declare a caliphate, was also reflected in both organizational and operational differences between the global jihadist movement's two heavyweights, the Islamic State and al-Qa'ida. The debate became so fierce that the Islamic State arrested the jihadi scholar Abu Ya'qub al-Maqdisi, a figure once described as the group's *mufti*.[63] Maqdisi's arrest, and the ongoing feud over the doctrine of takfir, threatened to undermine the ideological integrity of the organization and cast doubt on its ability to speak with one voice.[64] Furthermore, "a small but strident camp of hardliners consider Daesh's official ideology insufficiently radical and are pushing for an even more extremist stance that would exclude all possible cooperation with other jihadi groups, including al

---

[61] al-Masri, 2015, Ch. 7.

[62] al-Masri, 2015, Ch. 7.

[63] Abu Ya'qub al-Maqdisi is not be confused with Abu Muhammad al-Maqdisi, who influenced Zarqawi in Jordan (Cole Bunzel, "The Islamic State's Mufti on Trial: The Saga of 'Silsila 'Ilmiyya,'" *CTC Sentinel*, Vol. 11, No. 9, October 2018b). A *mufti* is an Islamic jurist who can issue a *fatwa*, an authoritative but nonbinding opinion, on Islamic law ("Mufti," in, 2003).

[64] Bunzel, 2018b.

Qaeda."[65] Some of the Islamic State's hard-core ideologues view the group's commitment to takfir as even more important than prayer and other fundamental components of Salafism.[66] Apparently, there is even a hard-core group of Islamic State militants, which Tore Hamming refers to as "the extremist wing of the Islamic State," that sees Baghdadi as "soft," leading to further fragmentation of the group.[67] Ideology will remain an important issue for the Islamic State, especially as the group seeks to transition into an underground insurgency and continue making money to buttress its organization and retain its capacity to plan and conduct attacks.

---

65 Rik Coolsaet, "Anticipating the Post-Daesh Landscape," Brussels: Egmont—The Royal Institute for International Relations, Egmont Paper 97, October 2017, p. 9. Daesh is the Arabic acronym for the Islamic State of Iraq and Syria, used as a pejorative.

66 R. Green, "Dispute Over Takfir Rocks Islamic State," Middle East Media Research Institute website, August 4, 2017.

67 Tore Hamming, "The Extremist Wing of the Islamic State," *Jihadica*, June 9, 2016.

CHAPTER THREE

Islamic State Revenues

The Islamic State's ability to sustain itself amid decline while rebuilding its organization to pursue its goals will depend in large part on its finances. Achieving its goals will require its ability to cover its day-to-day operating costs, salaries, military expenditures, administrative overhead, and many other miscellaneous costs it will incur. Although the one fact that many people remember about Islamic State finances is that it was the "richest terrorist group in the world" as it swept across Iraq and Syria in 2014 and 2015, the conventional-wisdom view in 2017 and 2018 was that its finances were in tatters, largely due to the loss of nearly all the territory it once controlled.[1]

Assessing the Islamic State's financial sustainability requires a two-pronged approach. The first is to look at basic trends in the Islamic State's estimated revenues. This can serve as a benchmark for progress against the group overall and establish a correlation between territorial contraction and a drastic reduction of revenue streams. However, these metrics were more useful for analyzing the Islamic State during the period that the Islamic State had a territorial caliphate than they are now that the Islamic State has reoriented itself mainly as an insur-

[1] In 2014, U.S. Under Secretary of Treasury for Terrorist Financing and Intelligence David Cohen called the Islamic State "probably the best-funded terrorist organization we have confronted" (David S. Cohen, "Attacking ISIL's Financial Foundation," remarks of Under Secretary for Terrorism and Financial Intelligence David S. Cohen at The Carnegie Endowment for International Peace, October 23, 2014a; see also Terrence McCoy, "ISIS Just Stole $425 Million, Iraqi Governor Says, and Became the 'World's Richest Terrorist Group,'" *Washington Post*, June 12, 2014).

gency.[2] The Islamic State has a different financial profile of basic revenues as an insurgency than it did in its peak period as a territorially based, statelike caliphate. This is true both of Islamic State revenues and expenditures in two ways: *requirements* and *types*. The group had different expenditure requirements when it was governing a territory than when it was acting as an insurgency. The group strove to provide at least a basic level of services to the population it governed when it held territory. It did not provide most of these services as an insurgency. Furthermore, different revenue types were available to it when it governed territory than when it was an insurgency. Control of populations expanded its taxation options and control of oil fields expanded its options from merely smuggling oil to extracting it and selling it overtly.

The second prong is to consider that the Islamic State's "business model" *after the caliphate* must be assessed based on different metrics that can tell us whether the group is likely to survive as an insurgency for the medium term (or longer) and whether its remaining leadership is capable of financing a future bid for resurgent territorial expansion, perhaps resembling a version of the group's blueprint to begin building a state through 2014. An extensive historical record that includes the Islamic State's own ledgers during periods in which it was both an insurgent and terrorist organization in decline can provide some clues. Moreover, remote-sensing analysis offers estimates of how Islamic State control affects numerous economic outcomes.[3] The historical evidence provides a useful lens through which to view how the Islamic State will act after the end of the territorial caliphate, particularly how it will

---

[2] Michael Knights, "Predicting the Shape of Iraq's Next Sunni Insurgencies," *CTC Sentinel*, Vol. 10, No. 7, August 2017; David Kilcullen, *Blood Year: Islamic State and the Failure of the War on Terror*, London: Hurst and Company, 2016; Hassan Hassan, *Out of the Desert: ISIS's Strategy for a Long War*, Washington, D.C.: Middle East Institute, Policy Paper 2018-8, September 2018c; Sarah AlMukhtar, Troy Griggs, K. K. Rebecca Lai, and Tim Wallace, "The Islamic State: From Insurgency to Rogue State and Back," *New York Times*, October 22, 2017.

[3] Robinson et al., 2017.

pursue its strategy of sustaining an insurgency, which offers the group more potential to regenerate its organization moving forward.[4]

In this chapter, we review the Islamic State's revenues through the group's historical iterations up to and including the fall of the caliphate and the group's resilience as an insurgency through early 2019. We provide background information on the group's financial capabilities at its peak, as well as its primary revenue sources while the group was at its high-water mark in 2014 and 2015 and how its revenue sources changed as it declined in 2016 and 2017, before retreating to remote areas and adopting an insurgency strategy in lieu of the territorial caliphate.

We start by examining trends from periods before the Islamic State's 2014 blitz, when the group's strategy involved engagement in clandestine activities that blended insurgency, terrorism, criminality, and state-building. That data were compiled at all, let alone as efficiently and in as routinize a way as they were, is suggestive of the group's bureaucratic resilience and capabilities. The data also enable a

---

[4] We use the terms *insurgency* and *terrorism* frequently in this report. Insurgency is often a type of alternative state-building in that insurgencies often tax local populations in areas under their control; provide at least some minimal services; and establish basic law-and-order institutions, such as auxiliary local police, paramilitary units, and justice systems. Terrorism, on the other hand, is a tactic that involves the use of politically motivated violence against noncombatants to cause intimidation or fear among a target audience. Most insurgent groups employ terrorism, but many terrorist groups are not insurgents because of the more expansive requirements to classify organized violence as an insurgency. See, for example, Stathis N. Kalyvas, *The Logic of Violence in Civil War*, New York: Cambridge University Press, 2006, pp. 245–246. For this research, we use a common definition of *insurgency* as "the organized use of subversion and violence to seize, nullify, or challenge political control of a region. Insurgency can also refer to the group itself" (Field Manual 3-24/Marine Corps Warfighting Publication 3-33.5, *Insurgencies and Countering Insurgencies*, Change 1, Washington, D.C.: Headquarters, Department of the Army, June 2014). Insurgent groups are nonstate organizations, although they may be more or less "statelike" organizations in fact. Insurgencies use violence and intimidation to pursue their aims. For various definitions of terrorism, see U.S. Department of State, Country Reports on Terrorism 2005, Washington, D.C.: Office of the Coordinator for Counterterrorism, April 2006, p. 9; Bruce Hoffman, *Inside Terrorism*, 2nd ed., New York: Columbia University Press, 2006, pp. 1–41; Robert A. Pape, *Dying to Win: The Strategic Logic of Suicide Terrorism*, New York: Random House, 2005, p. 9; and Audrey Kurth Cronin, "Behind the Curve: Globalization and International Terrorism," *International Security*, Vol. 27, No. 3, Winter 2002/03, p. 33.

window into what kind of budget the group might be able to sustain itself on, at what capacity, and whether and how the group has adapted its revenue-generating activities as a consequence of its changing organizational form, from a multidivisional statelike polity to an insurgency. Then, in the subsequent chapter, we complement this analysis by drawing on a unique set of interviews from the region to provide an on-the-ground view of the many ways that the Islamic State has raised revenue and why these mean it could continue to do so without holding much territory.

Islamic State Predecessor Group Financing

The Islamic State was renowned as "the richest terrorist group in the world" for much of 2014 and 2015 because it generated significant revenues from various sources and through innovative methods.[5] However, as discussed in Chapter One, the Islamic State has gone through a number of iterations. Throughout, it was guided by a central philosophy of raising money locally rather than seeking external donations, perhaps learning lessons from the counterthreat finance campaign against al-Qaʿida following the September 11, 2001, attacks.[6] In this section, we discuss revenue raising in two different periods of the Islamic State's predecessor groups: AQI in Anbar from May 2005 to December 2006 and ISI in Mosul from late 2008 through early 2009.

Revenue Totals of Predecessor Groups

Al-Qa'ida in Iraq in Anbar Governorate

A study of AQI's master financial ledgers for its Anbar provincial organization details exactly how the group's revenue can change over time.

---

[5] Christine Duhaime, *Terrorist Financing and the Islamic State*, white paper, Duhaime Law website, 2015; Michael Jonsson, *Funding the Islamic State: Sources of Revenue, Financing Requirements and Long-Term Vulnerabilities to Counter-Measures*, Stockholm: Swedish Defense Research Agency, December 2015; Tom Keatinge, "The Importance of Financing in Enabling and Sustaining the Conflict in Syria (and Beyond)," *Perspectives on Terrorism*, Vol. 8, No. 4, 2014.

[6] Bahney, Shatz, et al., 2010; Johnston, 2014; and Johnston et al., 2016.

The ledgers cover meticulously recorded, transaction-level revenue data for AQI in Anbar Governorate from June 2005 through November 2006, enabling uniquely comprehensive analysis of a terrorist group's finances and decisionmaking. The Anbar-based group's financials were documented by its top administrator, known as an "administrative emir." Due to a change in AQI administrative emirs in Anbar in May 2006, the group's financial record-keeping procedures changed slightly.

The first period corresponds to the administrative oversight of an administrative emir referred to in the captured documents as *Firas*, and the second corresponds to the administrative oversight of an administrative emir referred to as *'Imad*. Consequently, we divide AQI in Anbar's revenue totals into two distinct periods: June 2005 to May 2006 (Firas's administration) and June 2006 to November 2006 ('Imad's administration). From June 2005 to May 2006, AQI's Anbar administration raised nearly $4.5 million, or roughly $373,000 per month. AQI dramatically increased its revenues during the second period. Between June 2006 and November 2006, it raised $4.3 million, or roughly $860,000 per month.

Islamic State of Iraq in Ninewa Governorate

In addition to the documentary evidence on AQI's revenue stream and financial portfolio from Anbar Governorate, a second source of documentary evidence comes from ISI documents that were captured by Multi-National Coalition and Iraqi forces in 2009 and 2010 and were related to ISI revenues from Ninewa Governorate, where the city of Mosul is located. In Ninewa, the governorate's administrative emir, Ahmed Zayd, also known as Abu Zayd, tallied revenues on a single master spreadsheet for each month starting at the end of August 2008 and continuing through the end of January 2009.

During this period, although it maintained a clandestine presence in parts of Iraq, the group had been largely defeated and many of its leaders and members had been killed or imprisoned. Even so, the master ledgers contain records of $4.8 million in revenue, roughly $964,000 per month. Given the group's dramatic decline—both in territorial control and in attacks conducted—its ability to raise nearly $1 million per month demonstrates its financial resilience. As the number of ISI members decreased due to successful military and counterterrorism operations, it stands to reason that revenue per capita (for ISI members) increased after the group was forced from its Anbar stronghold and relocated to Mosul in 2008. Although we lack direct evidence on the group's revenue from internal ISI documents after February 2009, many sources indicate that the group managed to continue to increase its revenue streams.[7]

Revenue Sources of Predecessor Groups

The Islamic State's predecessor groups proved capable of generating revenue to finance its activities from a range of sources, which changed over time as the group's geographic terrain, military capabilities, and command-and-control structures shifted. AQI and ISI's financial ledgers from Anbar and Mosul show that the group's revenue sources changed over time and that the group was expert at adapting to changing circumstances.

Al-Qa'ida in Iraq in Anbar Governorate

From June 2005 to May 2006 (the period of Firas's administration), AQI's Anbar provincial administration classified revenue from stolen goods, spoils and loot or booty, car sales, and donations. It also recorded revenue to its central treasury as coming from its various sector administrations within the governorate but provided no further information on the sources of these sector revenues.[8] From June

---

[7] For example, the group reportedly was offering larger salaries than the Iraq government in mid-2010 to recruit members of the groups that had fought against it, suggesting it had ongoing revenue sources (Lister, 2014). Computer flash drives captured in June 2014 near Mosul showed that the Islamic State, then known as ISIS, had accumulated $875 million in total cash and assets (Chulov, 2014).

[8] When we discuss *spoils* and *loot or booty*, we are actually grouping two different concepts. The group used two different Arabic words for these revenue sources. The first is *ghana'im*, the plural of *ghanima*, which we translate as *spoils*, and which means wealth taken by force during a battle. The second is *fay'*, which we translate as *booty* or *loot*, and which means wealth taken from an enemy in peacetime or not in battle. For one definition of the Arabic term for spoils, see "Ghanimah," in Esposito, 2003. For one definition of the Arabic term for booty or loot, see "Fai," in Esposito, 2003. For a documentary example of the Arabic term

2006 to November 2006 (the period of 'Imad's administration), AQI's Anbar administration classified revenue as coming from spoils or looting and sales, transfers from sectors, and donations. We assess these sources to be about the same during both periods, although recategorized, with 'Imad grouping several categories that Firas had separated. In the second period, the percentage of revenue accounted for centrally by spoils, looting, and sales rose, and transfers from sectors fell proportionately, suggesting that the central administration took on a more important role in raising revenue. In both periods, donations constituted only a very small portion of the total: 5 percent in the first period and less than 3 percent in the second period. AQI records do not indicate the source of those donations.

Islamic State of Iraq in Ninewa Governorate

ISI in Ninewa in late 2008 and early 2009 obtained some $1.87 million (39 percent of its total revenue) from oil-related activities, such as gas stations and fuel-trucking companies it set up in Ninewa and elsewhere. The group also exploited the smuggling industry in Mosul and its surrounding environs. ISI tapped into these markets by taxing smugglers or reselling hijacked fuels, including gasoline, cooking gas, and diesel. The group's other major revenue source was extortion. According to the ISI records, its second-largest revenue source was extortion of contracted projects in and around Mosul, from which it generated almost $2 million over a five-month period, or 38 percent of the group's total revenue. This is a particular area of concern when considering an Islamic State resurgence in any future scenario involving reconstruction and the substantial sums of money allocated to such a Herculean task. Analysis of the ISI records from its time in Ninewa shows that the group did not extort the same amount of money each

---

for spoils, see the first entry on page 6 of the original Arabic version of the AQI document "Income and Outcome Report for Al-Anbar Province in Iraq 2," NMEC-2007-633700, 2006 (hosted on the Combating Terrorism Center at West Point website). For a documentary example of the Arabic term for loot or booty, see the Arabic entry on line 23 of page 2, referencing the sum of $7,500, of the original Arabic version of the AQI document, "Income and Outcome Report for Al-Anbar Province in Iraq 4," NMEC-2007-633919, 2006 (hosted on the Combating Terrorism Center at West Point website).

month. Extortion revenue fluctuated month by month and declined overall in the period studied. At one point, senior ISI leadership sought to increase revenue by co-opting Sunni politicians at the local and national levels with the authority to make budget allocations that ISI could tap.[9]

Predecessor Group Revenues: Implications for the Islamic State

Two lessons can be learned about the Islamic State's finances from its history. First, both of its earlier incarnations illustrate that the group financed itself from local sources where it operated, regardless of whether it controlled territory or maintained some other type of presence. Furthermore, its actions illustrate the types of revenue-raising activities in which it engaged when it was more of an insurgency rather than a territorial ruler, including extortion, smuggling, and a variety of other criminal activities.

Second, the cases also illustrate that the group governed its finances by establishing and maintaining a hierarchical organization capable of centralizing control over revenues and expenses through its internal governance structures while still delegating responsibility for revenue generation and expense tracking to lower-level financial and administrative emirs. This delegation took place at both the governorate and sector levels and provided significant autonomy to these lower-level units. A 2008 "lessons learned" document captured from ISI provides a useful illustration of the importance of effective financial management for the group's operations. The author noted the importance of centralizing finances to redistribute money to units that had limited revenues or large expenses. The document also makes a case for the importance of diversified local revenue streams as a hedge against negative economic shocks, a feat not easily achieved by a nonstate actor, yet something that ISI accomplished. It warns about the vulnerabilities associated with a reliance on funding from a foreign state sponsor; such funding to jihadi organizations had come at the whims of foreign

---

[9] Benjamin Bahney, Patrick B. Johnston, and Patrick Ryan, "The Enemy You Know and the Ally You Don't," *Foreign Policy*, June 23, 2015.

intelligence services and could be terminated at any time, leaving them at risk of collapse.[10]

From a historical perspective, the two previous incarnations provide useful variation in the group's size and strength, the extent of territorial control, its top leadership, its primary operating locations within Iraq and Syria, and a host of other factors. Examining the extent to which Islamic State financing has evolved can help us to compare and contrast the group's financial well-being and its methods of financing over time and thus inform us about how the group is likely to behave and perform financially in the future in various environments and scenarios.

Islamic State Revenues, 2014–2017

The Islamic State's total revenue rose from a little less than $1 million per month in late 2008 and early 2009 to between $1 million to $3 million per day in 2014.[11] In November 2014 congressional testimony on Islamic State financing, a former U.S. Department of the Treasury official and an expert on terrorist financing noted that "by September [2014], estimates put ISIS's daily income at around $3 million, giving it a total value of assets between $1.3 and $2 billion, making it the world's best-funded terrorist group."[12] During the group's rise as a territorial power, some indications suggested that it was an adversary on par with "normal countries" based on several geographic, military, and financial dimensions. A September 2014 *Washington Post* article that compared the Islamic State with sovereign countries indicated that the group was roughly the same size geographically as Great Britain; was up to one-third larger than Madagascar in terms of military man-

---

[10] "Analysis of the State of ISI," undated, p. 23; Brian Fishman, *Dysfunction and Decline: Lessons Learned from Inside Al Qa'ida in Iraq*, West Point, N.Y.: Combating Terrorism Center at West Point, March 16, 2009.

[11] Johnston, 2014, pp. 2–3.

[12] Matthew Levitt, "Terrorist Financing and the Islamic State," testimony submitted to the House Committee on Financial Services, November 13, 2014.

power; and was producing up to 40 percent more barrels per day of oil than Bahrain.[13]

Although there has been little similarly comprehensive research on Islamic State revenues after 2010 compared to what had been done on the revenues of the group before 2010, the group appears to have built significantly on the revenue streams it was exploiting until the beginning of its 2014 offensive in Iraq. Financial data recovered from a then-ISIS courier's thumb drive reportedly indicated that the group had a net surplus of $875 million.[14] This would mean that the group had increased its revenues from perhaps a few million dollars per month as of January 2010 to an average of about $20 million per month in subsequent months until June 2014, when the courier's financial data were obtained. The group's records as AQI and ISI indicated that spending was about on par with revenues. Therefore, for simplicity's sake, we can assume a net balance of zero as of February 2010 and divide the reported $875 million by the 41 months between February 2010 and June 2014 for an average net surplus of $21.3 million per month. Given its mounting military operations during the period and its accumulation of members, the group likely was earning far more than that in monthly revenue, well above what it had gained in its earlier operating periods.

This also represents an important change in the group's financial activities. As noted above, from 2005 through 2010, ledgers indicated that expenses were close to revenues and that the group did not hold surpluses. This surplus post-2010 made the group more dangerous than it had been because it increased the group's freedom of action

---

[13] *The Washington Post* reported that the Islamic State was producing between 30,000 and 70,000 barrels per day, while Bahrain was producing 40,000 barrels per day. The paper also reported revenue estimates of "$300 million +" for the Islamic State and "$308 million" for the Vatican. See Rick Noack, "Here's How the Islamic State Compares with Real States," *Washington Post*, September 12, 2014.

[14] Ian Black, Rania Abouzeid, Mark Tran, Shiraz Maher, Roger Tooth, and Martin Chulov, "The Terrifying Rise of Isis: $2bn in Loot, Online Killings and an Army on the Run," *Guardian*, June 16, 2014; Sarah Almukhtar, "ISIS Finances Are Strong," *New York Times*, May 19, 2015; Basma Salama, *The Resilience of the Islamic State*, Republik Österreich: Bundesministerium für Landesverteidigung und Sport, 2016, p. 37.

in terms of paying personnel, buying equipment, bribing officials, or funding other insurgent activities.

In addition to the $875 million the Islamic State had when it moved on Mosul in June 2014, it seized between $500 million and $1 billion more, in cash and gold from bank vaults and from the property of citizens who fled in anticipation of the group's wrath upon its arrival.[15] As of 2014, the group's total assets were estimated at $2 billion.[16] Despite their high value, these assets were not renewable revenue sources. Their seizure by the Islamic State was achieved through a series of one-off incidents. As the group conquered new territory—it continued to expand into 2015—its soldiers confiscated assets under the guidance of their leader and allocated them initially to the Islamic State's Treasury Department [*Bayt al-Mal*].[17]

After the group's territorial expansion ground to a halt, it no longer gained the large capital infusions that propelled the group's expansion from 2013 through late 2015. Still, in addition to reserves of $2 billion or more, the Islamic State's aggressive approach to state-building fostered the creation of surprisingly strong institutions—and, in many cases, the group's co-optation and coercion of extant local institutions, structures, physical infrastructure, and human capital.[18] The Islamic State targeted its use of coercion and inducement toward labor in industries whose functioning and performance required the recruitment and retention of skilled labor. Included were industries the Islamic State designated as "strategic," such as the oil and gas industries, as well as those that required specialized expertise or technical knowledge, such as Islamic State–controlled hydroelectric dams, hos-

---

15 Eckart Woertz, "How Long Will ISIS Last Economically?" Barcelona Centre for International Affairs, Notes Internacionals CIDOB No. 98, October 2014, p. 3.

16 Chulov, 2014; Woertz, 2014.

17 Hassan Abu Hanieh and Mohammad Abu Rumman, *The Islamic State Organization: The Sunni Crisis and the Struggle of Global Jihadism*, trans. Banan Malkawi, Amman, Jordan: Friedrich Ebert Stiftung, 2015, pp. 277–279.

18 See Aymenn Jawad al-Tamimi, "The Evolution in Islamic State Administration: The Documentary Evidence," *Perspectives on Terrorism*, Vol. 9, No. 4, October 2015b; Aymenn al-Tamimi, "A Caliphate Under Strain: The Documentary Evidence," *CTC Sentinel*, Vol. 9, No. 4, April 2016b, pp. 1–8; Hassan, 2018c; and Robinson et al., 2017, pp. 10–14.

pitals, and schools.[19] Where the Islamic State controlled territory, state-like institutions regulated predominant sectors of the economy, including agriculture, trade, industrial activities, real estate, tax collection, immigration, and customs enforcement at border crossings. The group also boasted an intelligence capability combined with law enforcement institutions that were endowed with the authority to impose fees on citizens for putative moral violations under the caliphate's laws.

How much revenue did the Islamic State bring in during its years as a territorial caliphate? The group generated substantial top-line revenues from 2014 to 2017. Most of these revenues were generated from local sources, within the expansive Islamic State–controlled territory that sprawled across large parts of Iraq and Syria. Although existing estimates of Islamic State revenues lack precision due to information gaps—a comprehensive understanding of Islamic State revenues is impossible without fuller access to the group's financial documents, especially its master financial ledgers—estimates are available on total revenue and types of revenue sources (Table 3.1).

Islamic State revenue peaked in 2014 or 2015, depending on the preferred estimate. Most of the reporting for 2014 concurred that the group's revenue that year was between $1 billion and $3 billion. Although the group controlled parts of Anbar Governorate as early as 2012 and 2013, its 2014 offensives, in which it seized the city of Mosul and other population centers in Salah-al Din and Anbar governorates in Iraq, as well as oil- and gas-producing regions in eastern and central Syria, catapulted its revenue-generating capacity.

The extent of the Islamic State's control of the populations and territory peaked in late 2014 and 2015, partly because it plundered state institutions, private property, and natural resources. In many areas, including Mosul—the "financial capital" of the caliphate, due to its size and economic importance—the Islamic State imposed new regula-

---

[19] In and around Raqqa, for instance, former municipal workers being paid by the Islamic State staffed hydroelectric power-generation facilities at the Tabqah, Ba'ath, and Tishreen Dams (Umar Farooq, "Raqqa: 'It Is a Very Sad Life Under ISIL,'" Al Jazeera, January 28, 2015).

Table 3.1
Estimated Islamic State Revenues, by Year, U.S. $ Millions

Year	Low	Medium	High
2014	970	1,890	2,900
2015	1,035	1,700	2,400
2016	520	870	870
2017	192	192	192

SOURCES: Adam Szubin, "Remarks by Acting Under Secretary Adam Szubin at Chatham House," Washington, D.C.: U.S. Department of the Treasury, December 10, 2015; Daniel Glaser, "Testimony of A\S for Terrorist Financing Daniel Glaser Before the House Committee on Foreign Affairs Subcommittee on Terrorism, Nonproliferation, and Trade and the House Committee on Armed Services Subcommittee on Emerging Threats and Capabilities," Washington, D.C.: U.S. Department of the Treasury, June 9, 2016b; Fanusie and Entz, 2017; Stefan Heißner, Peter R. Neumann, John Holland-McCowan, and Rajan Basra, "Caliphate in Decline: An Estimate of Islamic State's Financial Fortunes," London: International Centre for the Study of Radicalisation, 2017; IHS Markit, "Islamic State Monthly Revenue Drops to $56 Million, IHS Says," press release, April 18, 2016; IHS Markit, "Islamic State Territory Down 60 Percent and Revenue Down 80 Percent on Caliphate's Third Anniversary, IHS Markit Says," press release, June 29, 2017; Erika Solomon, Guy Chazan, and Sam Jones, "ISIS Inc.: How Oil Fuels the Jihadi Terrorists," *Financial Times*, October 14, 2015; Erika Solomon and Sam Jones, "ISIS Inc.: Loot and Taxes Keep Jihadi Economy Churning," *Financial Times*, December 14, 2015; Almukhtar, 2015; Jean-Charles Brisard and Damien Martinez, *Islamic State: The Economy-Based Terrorist Funding*, ThomsonReuters Accelus, October 2014; Laurence Bindner and Gabriel Poirot, *ISIS Financing in 2015*, Paris: Center for the Analysis of Terrorism, May 2016; Colin P. Clarke, Kimberly Jackson, Patrick B. Johnston, Eric Robinson, Howard J. Shatz, *Financial Futures of the Islamic State of Iraq and the Levant: Findings from a RAND Corporation Workshop*, Santa Monica, Calif.: RAND Corporation, CF-361, 2017; Financial Action Task Force, *Financing of the Terrorist Organization Islamic State in Iraq and the Levant*, Paris, 2015.

NOTES: Various sources were consulted to provide a generic overview from extant reporting of Islamic State revenue trends over time across three categories of revenue estimates: a low, a medium, and a high estimate. The low is the lowest reported believable number, the high is the highest reported believable number, and the medium is a reported, in-between number.

tions, taxes, fees, and fines on the populations living under its control, creating new revenue-generating opportunities.

Revenue began to decline in 2016: The low-end estimate is more than $500 million, and the high-end estimate is $870 million—still a good deal of revenue for a group reportedly in trouble with its finances.

Revenues continued to decrease through 2017 as the Islamic State lost nearly all its territory by the end of the year. Still, IHS Markit analysts projected the group's 2017 revenue at $192 million, as of 2017's second quarter.[20] It was expected that the group's revenue would continue to decline in 2018. Indeed, an announcement from the coalition fighting the Islamic State, Operation Inherent Resolve, reported that Islamic State oil revenues decreased to $4 million per month as of late 2017.[21]

Territorial and Population Control and Islamic State Revenue

It is useful to consider these revenue totals while also accounting for changes in the amount of territory and the estimated population living in the territory the Islamic State controlled over time to assess the relationship between estimated revenue and the expanse of the group's territorial and population control. Numerous analysts have linked the decline in Islamic State–controlled territory, and the population within that territory, starting in 2016 to a concomitant decline in group revenues.[22]

By early 2015, the Islamic State had captured more than 90,000 km^2 of territory (Table 3.2). It continued to expand its territorial control, reaching a peak later that year of 104,000 km^2, or 16.7 percent of Iraq and Syria. Table 3.3 shows the total land area of Iraq and Syria.

The Islamic State gained sizable amounts of revenue from taxing the people within its territory, so it is important to consider population as well. The Islamic State held large amounts of sparsely populated desert in the run-up to its conquests. Once it started conquering cities, population rose. Given the conquest of cities, Islamic State population also peaked between late 2014 and mid-2015 (Table 3.4). Population

---

20 IHS Markit, 2017.

21 Reported in Jim Michaels, "U.S. Coalition Slashes ISIS Oil Revenue by More Than 90%," *USA Today*, October 2, 2017. For further analysis of Islamic State oil revenue through early 2018, specifically trends in airstrikes and Islamic State oil revenue, see Matthew Reed, "ISIS Is Out of the Oil Business," *Fuse*, March 27, 2018.

22 Merrit Kennedy, "New Report Finds ISIS Territorial Defeats Are Also Hitting the Group's Wallet," National Public Radio, February 21, 2017; Charles Riley, "ISIS Is Losing Mosul and Most of Its Income," CNN Money website, June 29, 2017.

Table 3.2
Estimated Islamic State–Controlled Territory in Iraq and Syria

	Islamic State–Controlled Territory		
Period	**km²**	**% of Iraq and Syria**	**Sources**
January 2015	90,800	14.6	Jon Greenberg, "Donald Trump: ISIS Territory Losses Near 100 Percent," Politifact website, January 30, 2018
First half of 2015	104,000	16.7	Rukmini Callimachi, "In an email, US-backed Coalition fighting ISIS told me that of the 104,000 square kms the group held in Iraq/Syria, 93,790 is liberated," tweet, October 17, 2017[a]
October 2017	10,210	1.6	Callimachi, 2017[a]

[a] Source does not provide a date for territorial control of 104,000 km^2. However, alternative sources indicate that the Islamic State lost territory through the first half of 2015, so we infer that its peak came during that first half (e.g., Columb Strack, "Islamic State Territory Shrinks by 9.4% in First Six Months of 2015," *Jane's Intelligence Review*, July 28, 2015).

estimates are not always consistent, especially because the last Syrian census was held in 2004 and because the last Iraqi census was held in 1987. In addition, the high numbers of refugees and displaced people have made estimating population in Islamic State territory difficult. But the general trend is clear. At its peak, the population living in Islamic State territory amounted to about 17 percent of the total Iraqi and Syrian population, about the same proportion as of land held.[23]

Given the control of territory and population, the period from late 2014 through mid-2015 was by far the Islamic State's most successful for making money. As it blitzed through new territory and raised the black flag that signified Islamic State sovereignty, its soldiers looted, pillaged, and extorted. And then it settled down to govern. It experienced major territorial and population reversals through 2017, especially with its loss of Mosul, Iraq's second-largest city, in July 2017 and its loss of Raqqa, Syria, in October 2017.

[23] Iraq and Syria population data are midyear estimates for 2015 from U.S. Census, International Data Base, rev. September 18, 2018.

Table 3.3
Total Land Area of Iraq and Syria

Location	Total Land Area (km^2)	Share of Combined Iraq and Syria (%)	Source
Iraq	438,317	70.3	"Iraq Country Profile," BBC News website, October 3, 2018
Syria	185,180	29.7	"Syria Country Profile," BBC, April 24, 2018.
Total	623,497	100.0	

Table 3.4
Estimated Population in Islamic State–Controlled Territory

Period	Syria (millions)	Iraq (millions)	Iraq and Syria (millions)	Source
November 2014			5–6	UNSC, Letter Dated 13 November 2014 from the Chair of the Security Council Committee Pursuant to Resolutions 1267 (1999) and 1989 (2011) Concerning Al-Qaida and Associated Individuals and Entities Addressed to the President of the Security Council, S/2014/815, November 14, 2014b
January 2015			9	IHS Markit, 2016[a]
April 2015	2.7			Lead Inspector General for Overseas Contingency Operations, *Operation Inherent Resolve: Quarterly Report and Biannual Report to the United States Congress, September 30, 2015*, December 3, 2015b
June 2015	2.7			Lead Inspector General for Overseas Contingency Operations, *Operation Inherent Resolve: Quarterly Report to the United States Congress, April 1, 2015–June 30, 2015*, August 24, 2015a
July 2015			8	United Nations, "In ISIL-Controlled Territory, 8 Million Civilians Living In 'State of Fear'—UN Expert," UN News website, July 31, 2015a

Table 3.4—Continued

Period	Syria (millions)	Iraq (millions)	Iraq and Syria (millions)	Source
March 2016		3		Lead Inspector General for Overseas Contingency Operations, *Operation Inherent Resolve: Quarterly Report to the United States Congress, March 31, 2016*, May 6, 2016
April 2016			6	IHS Markit, 2016[a]
December 2016		3		Lead Inspector General for Overseas Contingency Operations, *Operation Inherent Resolve: Quarterly Report to the United States Congress, October 1, 2016–December 31, 2016*, February 2, 2017a

NOTES: Data are not necessarily consistent across geographies, given different estimation methods, lack of strong knowledge of precaliphate populations, and population changes due to refugees and the internally displaced.

[a] Estimates are based on the statement in the source that "The Islamic State has lost about 22 percent of its territory in the past 15 months . . . . Its population has declined from around nine million to around six million."

The group proved to be capable of performing some basic governance functions, especially in cities in which its support structure was most deeply embedded—Raqqa and Mosul—but metrics of various types of economic activity declined substantially, on average, after it assumed control over a city.[24] In 2015, the Islamic State's expansion stalled. It had indeed achieved its goal of building a state and now had to contend with a state that had grown costly to maintain. Further, in the face of an increasingly effective counter–Islamic State military campaign being fought on multiple fronts by a myriad of actors, including powerful state security forces and nonstate militias alike, the Islamic State's revenue-collection ability finally reached its limits.

But just as it had behaved between 2007 and 2010, when it was on the defensive, the Islamic State adapted. The group stopped recruiting

24 Robinson et al., 2017.

foreign fighters, cut salaries by 50 percent across the organization—an enormous cut in the group's payroll—and discontinued or charged more for many of the services it already provided.[25] Consequently, the size of the organization decreased along with the amounts being paid for salaries. Likewise, leadership effectively sought to shutter some of its administrative functions, advising commanders in writing to send certain administrators from the back office to the front line to fight.

Despite these dramatic reversals of the Islamic State's financial fortunes, it managed to take on a new shape as an insurgency.[26] After this reorganization, it positioned itself to remain financially solvent and capable of financing a sustained resurgence should favorable conditions arise. When it lost the battles of Mosul and of Raqqa, many of its operatives dispersed. Some returned to their home countries or migrated to other jihadist theaters, including the Philippines, Libya, and Afghanistan. But thousands stayed, and some formed cells in various cities.[27] In the Euphrates River Valley in eastern Syria, the Islamic State maintained control of territory amounting to about 10 percent of what it controlled at its peak, according to a spokesman for the multinational coalition battling the Islamic State in 2018. The group retained pockets of control and influence in some key areas of the Euphrates River Valley in and around Mayadin city and in the Syria-Iraq border cities of Albu Kamal, Syria, and al-Qaim, Iraq, to name the most notable holdouts.[28] For the Islamic State, the deserts of the provinces it called

---

[25] Jose Pagliery, "ISIS Cuts Its Fighters' Salaries by 50%," CNN, January 19, 2016; Al-Tamimi, 2016b.

[26] Hassan Hassan, "ISIS Is Poised to Make a Comeback in Syria," *Atlantic*, September 18, 2018d.

[27] Hassan Hassan, "ISIS Is Ready for a Resurgence," *Atlantic*, August 26, 2018b.

[28] Islamic State members who remained in the eastern Syria desert appeared to be heeding Islamic State spokesman and external operations chief Abu Muhammad al-Adnani's advice to return to the desert to continue the jihad. See commentary on Adnani's speech and its implications for Islamic State strategy in Hassan Hassan, "The Islamic State After Mosul," *New York Times*, October 24, 2016b. See also Abu Muhammad al-Adnani ash-Shami, "That They Live By Proof," AlHayat Media Center, 2016. The original document was accessed at Pieter Van Ostaeyen, "Pietervanostaeyn: Musings on Arabism, Islamicism, History, and Current Affairs," website, undated.

Jazirah and al-Furat are no less important than Mosul.[29] Indeed, as the analyst Hassan Hassan observed, "For long-term survival, the desert matters as much as the cities. Wilayat al-Furat is the only province that crosses the Iraq-Syria border and the territory and remote areas like it are potential hide-outs for senior members—if they are not there already."[30] Throughout this period of decline, the Islamic State continued to generate revenues locally and retained substantial reserves, perhaps much as it did in 2012 and 2013, just before the phase of territorial and population expansion.

Causes of Declining Revenue, 2016–2018

Although the Islamic State maintained financial self-sufficiency after losing territory, its transition to insurgency coincided with a significant decline in total revenue in late 2017 and over the course of 2018. Precise estimates of total revenue generated in this period are elusive because of the group's move underground and its attendant switch to covert financing methods.

The decline in Islamic State revenue, which began in late 2015 and continued through 2018, resulted from countermeasures that targeted several of the group's main revenue sources. These countermeasures included

- bombing Islamic State oil and gas assets and supply chain
- reducing the Islamic State's tax base by rolling back its territorial gains
- bombing the Islamic State's bulk cash facilities
- reducing the Islamic State's access to the formal financial system
- targeting and killing financial leadership.

---

[29] Brian Dodwell, Daniel Milton, and Muhammad Al-'Ubaydi, "Burying the Lede: The Islamic State Downsizes?" Combating Terrorism Center at West Point website, July 20, 2018; Michael Weiss and Hassan Hassan, "How to Salvage Syria," *Daily Beast*, December 7, 2016.

[30] Hassan, 2016b.

Oil: The Coalition Air Campaign and Operation Tidal Wave II

Although the Islamic State's finances remained strong through 2015, the group started to suffer a major reversal of its financial fortunes toward the end of that year with an aggressive U.S. air campaign carried out against oil assets, named Tidal Wave II (after Operation Tidal Wave, a U.S. air campaign against oil infrastructure in Romania during World War II).[31] According to U.S. officials, the operational concept that underlay Operation Tidal Wave II was informed by an intelligence trove captured in a May 2015 raid that killed Islamic State minister of oil Abu Sayyaf. The captured electronic media contained detailed information about the inner workings of the group's oil operations. That information, according to these officials, helped the U.S.-led coalition better understand the limitations of previous military operations, which consisted mostly of the use of airpower against Islamic State mobile oil refineries. The coalition expanded the air campaign against oil assets to go after the entire supply chain from which the Islamic State could profit.[32] The targeting included airstrikes against oil fields, refineries, and tanker trucks and other assets encompassing much of the Islamic State oil and gas supply chain. The targeting took place in both Syria and Iraq. For example, in June 2016, coalition airstrikes destroyed an Islamic State Ministry of Oil headquarters in Mosul.[33]

Information released from the Abu Sayyaf documents indicated that his organization controlled 253 oil wells throughout Syria. Oil expert Matthew Reed estimated that, by October 2016, coalition airstrikes had destroyed 224 of them, although some may have been

---

[31] Adam Szubin, "Remarks of Acting Under Secretary Adam Szubin on Countering the Financing of Terrorism at the Paul H. Nitze School of Advanced International Studies," Washington, D.C.: U.S. Department of the Treasury, October 20, 2016.

[32] Joby Warrick and Liz Sly, "U.S.-Led Strikes Putting a Financial Squeeze on the Islamic State," *Washington Post*, April 2, 2016; Joby Warrick, "Satellite Photos Show Islamic State Installing Hundreds of Makeshift Oil Refineries to Offset Losses from Airstrikes," *Washington Post*, July 7, 2016.

[33] U.S. Central Command, "Military Airstrikes Continue Against ISIL Terrorists in Syria and Iraq," press release, June 23, 2016.

reconstituted.[34] By May 2016, the U.S.-led coalition estimated that the Islamic State's oil revenues had been cut by about 50 percent.[35] That same month, a U.S. Department of the Treasury official noted that Islamic State oil revenues had likely decreased from almost $500 million per year to about $250 million per year.[36]

One other notable factor that limited Islamic State oil revenues was the hardening of the once porous Syria-Turkey border.[37] Turkey finally increased its efforts to stop the flow of people, materiel, and money crossing its border with Syria, restricting the Islamic State's ability to sell oil there. Securing the border was daunting and imperfect, but Turkey's greater level of commitment to border security, which came in the wake of terrorist attacks in some of its major cities, forced the Islamic State to sell the majority of its oil in local markets and at depressed prices through 2016 and 2017. While the Syria-Turkey border is unlikely ever to be fully secure, greater political effort to use Turkey's military and law enforcement along the border clearly helped deter smugglers and traffickers from crossing back and forth with impunity.

Tax Revenue Decreased as the Territorial Caliphate Contracted

Taxation and extortion were among the Islamic State's largest sources of revenue. The group taxed most economic activities it could monitor, affecting the economic activities of the millions of people once under its control.[38] According to a UK government official (and as described in more detail in the next chapter),

> Broadly, I would say look at any aspect of the economy and where it's easy to regulate or you can calculate, they have tax inspectors

---

[34] Matthew Reed, "Blowing Up the Islamic State's Oil Company," *Foreign Policy*, October 26, 2016.

[35] Pellerin, 2016.

[36] Yeganeh Torbati, "Islamic State Yearly Oil Revenue Halved to $250 Million: U.S. Official," Reuters, May 11, 2016.

[37] Louisa Loveluck, "Anger and Fear Along Turkey's Border as Offensive Brings the War Back Home," *Washington Post*, February 7, 2018.

[38] Bindner and Poirot, 2016, pp. 14–18.

> and they go out and they assess how much crop can come from a field. So if you had an industry that was quite easy to observe, they were very good at taxing it.[39]

Estimates of Islamic State revenue from taxation and extortion vary considerably because of the extreme difficulty of accessing representative data on the group's income from taxes, extortion, and other fees. According to a senior U.S. Department of the Treasury official, the Islamic State made $350 million or $360 million in annual tax revenue during its peak years.[40] As it lost oil revenue and territory, the group became more heavily dependent on the population over which it retained influence for revenue.[41] One estimate held that the group's revenue from taxation had fallen by almost 80 percent since 2015.[42]

After the fall of Raqqa, the Islamic State found itself largely relegated to locations in remote deserts and in towns in and around the Euphrates River Valley near the Syria-Iraq border or in small, clandestine cells in towns and cities in both Iraq and Syria.[43] This severely hobbled its ability to overtly tax people and business activities. The group, however, has retained the ability to generate revenue through criminality: It remains ensconced in the region's smuggling networks; is able to extort oil and other commercial activities; and, possibly, has large sums of money stashed abroad thanks to transfers the group carried out to protect its assets when the caliphate began to collapse.[44] We discuss these revenue sources further later.

---

[39] Alexander Lewis, "Coalition Hopes to Use ISIL's Own Tax Regime Against It," Tax Notes International website, May 2, 2016.

[40] Torbati, 2016; Glaser, 2016b.

[41] Ahmed Rasheed, "Islamic State's Oil Revenue Dives as it Loses Iraqi Territory," Reuters, July 28, 2016.

[42] IHS Markit, 2017.

[43] Hassan Hassan, "ISIL Sleeper Cells in Iraq Are a Warning Sign the Extremist Group Is Already Reforming," *National*, March 28, 2018a.

[44] See, for example, Renad Mansour and Hisham al-Hashimi, "ISIS and the New War Economy," Chatham House website, June 8, 2017. See also Renad Mansour and Hisham al-Hashimi, "ISIS Is Still in Business," Chatham House website, January 17, 2018.

Destroying Bulk Cash Facilities

In addition to attacking the Islamic State's oil and natural gas supply chain, a separate line of effort, called Operation Point Blank, targeted Islamic State cash directly, going after the sites at which the group stored its cash.[45] The first reported strike against cash storage took place in Mosul in January 2016, with initial reports of "tens of millions of dollars" destroyed.[46] One notable series of strikes in Mosul was reported to have destroyed branches of the Iraqi Central Bank, the state-owned al-Rasheed Bank, al-Aqari Bank, and Abu Tammam Bank.[47] Further strikes on cash storage facilities continued through at least mid-2017. As of March 2017, the coalition had conducted 25 such strikes. In late July or early August 2017, the coalition destroyed a bulk cash deposit at Albu Kamal. The coalition put the amount overall at "tens of millions—and possibly hundreds of millions—of dollars."[48]

Measures Related to Financial Institutions and the Global Financial System

The coalition and its Iraqi government partner took other financial steps. Iraq had been sending approximately $170 million per month to its government employees in Islamic State territory in 2015, or the equivalent of $2 billion per year, and the Islamic State had been taxing the transfers. By the summer of 2015, the government of Iraq decided to ban and hold in escrow the distribution of these government salaries.

---

[45] Pellerin, 2016.

[46] Jim Miklaszewski and Corky Siemaszko, "Millions in ISIS Cash Destroyed in U.S. Airstrike," NBC News, January 11, 2016. For information on subsequent airstrikes, see Patrick B. Johnston, "Islamic State's Money Problems," *USA Today*, March 4, 2016, and Matthew Rosenberg, "U.S. Drops Bombs Not Just on ISIS, But on Its Cash, Too," *New York Times*, January 20, 2016.

[47] Jack Moore, "U.S.-Led Coalition Targets ISIS Banks in Mosul Strikes," *Newsweek*, February 15, 2016.

[48] For the report of 25 strikes and the dollar estimate, see U.S. Department of State, "The Global Coalition—Working to Defeat ISIS," fact sheet, Washington, D.C.: Office of the Spokesperson, March 22, 2017. For the strike in Albu Kamal, which also included the destruction of an Islamic State financial headquarters, see Cheryl Pellerin, "OIR Spokesman: No Safe Havens Left for ISIS in Syria or Iraq," DoD News website, August 10, 2017.

The U.S. Department of the Treasury and members of the Global Coalition Against the Islamic State worked with the Central Bank of Iraq to identify financial institutions that the Islamic State could have been using. As a result, the government of Iraq cut off 90 bank branches within Islamic State territory from both the international and Iraqi banking systems, and the Central Bank of Iraq banned 150 exchange houses and money-transfer companies from participation in its dollar auctions.[49]

Further on the multilateral front, the Counter-ISIL Finance Group (now the Counter-ISIS Finance Group)—co-led by Italy, Saudi Arabia, and the United States and, as of September 2018, comprising 52 member states and organizations—worked to prevent the Islamic State from using the international financial system. This group conducted its work in coordination with the multilateral Financial Action Task Force, the intergovernmental standard-setting body for anti–money laundering and countering the financing of terrorism.

In addition, the United States and Iraq established the Bilateral Commission to Counter Terrorist Financing, focused on information and intelligence exchanges. The United States sanctioned numerous senior leaders, financiers, foreign terrorist fighter facilitators, and Islamic State branches. And the United Nations passed UNSC Resolution 2253 in December 2015, which added the Islamic State to existing al-Qa'ida sanctions to cement multilateral cooperation to counter Islamic State financing.[50]

Financial Leadership Decapitation

Airstrikes have successfully targeted important individuals, killing a number of high-ranking financial and oil officials, as exemplified by the death of Abu Sayyaf discussed earlier. Over three months in 2015, coalition airstrikes killed three members of the Islamic State's

---

[49] Counter ISIL Finance Group, "Fact Sheet: Taking Stock of the Counter ISIL Finance Group's Achievements in its First Year," April 8, 2016. This can also be found with a description of the Counter ISIL Finance Group meeting at U.S. Department of the Treasury, "United States, Italy, and the Kingdom of Saudi Arabia Hold Fourth Plenary of the Counter-ISIL Finance Group in Rome," press release, Washington, D.C., April 11, 2016a.

[50] UNSC, Resolution 2253, December 17, 2015.

finance network, culminating in the death of Abu Saleh, the finance minister, in November 2015.[51] In April 2016, the coalition killed Abd al-Rahman al-Qaduli, also known as Haji Iman, among other names, also identified as a minister of finance.[52]

Later that year, the Kurdistan Region Security Council announced a joint operation between the Iraqi Kurdistan Counter Terrorism forces and U.S. Special Forces that killed Sami Jasim Mohammed Al-Jabouri, known as Haji Hamad, responsible for all natural resources in Iraq and Syria.[53] And in June 2017, coalition forces killed Islamic State financial facilitator Fawaz Muhammad Jubayr al-Rawi, whom the U.S. Department of the Treasury had previously designated for sanctions as the owner of the Hanifa money exchange in Albu Kamal, from which he moved money into and out of Islamic State territory.[54]

Conclusions About Causes of Declining Islamic State Revenues

A confluence of factors contributed to the decline in Islamic State revenues starting in late 2015. Some depended on the fact that the group controlled territory and so may have little application to ongoing efforts against the group. These included retaking oil fields, striking oil infrastructure it controlled, and limiting its ability to tax by retaking territory. Others, however, remain applicable. These include senior leader strikes and strikes against cash storage facilities. However, the group has proved resourceful in the past and, as its record from 2006 through 2013 shows, is capable of continuing to raise revenue even while under attack.

The Islamic State demonstrated this resourcefulness as it lost its territorial caliphate in 2017. Before coalition forces liberated Raqqa,

---

[51] Steve Warren, "Department of Defense Press Briefing by Col. Warren," Operation Inherent Resolve Spokesman, December 10, 2015.

[52] Lead Inspector General for Overseas Contingency Operations, 2016, p. 10.

[53] Kurdistan Region Security Council, "Joint Op by our Counter Terrorism Dept (CTD) & U.S. Special forces killed snr #ISIL member near Iraqi-Syrian border," press release via Twitter, Office of the Chancellor, August 11, 2016.

[54] CJTF-OIR PAO, "Coalition Forces Kill ISIS Financial Facilitator," press release, June 23, 2017.

Syria, Islamic State enforcers issued fines, instead of administering corporal punishments, to accumulate money and forced residents to swap currency for Islamic State–issued money.[55] Even with losses of territory, the Islamic State still controlled some oil infrastructure heading into late 2017 and was earning somewhere between $4 million and $10 million per month through oil trading, amounting to $36 million to $120 million per year.[56]

New Revenue Sources After the Caliphate

Despite the collapse of the territorial caliphate, the Islamic State has displayed resilience and commitment, signaling a resolve that could help the group engineer a comeback even long after the removal of its state. In a sign of its organizational resilience, as of mid-2018, the Islamic State's security and finance structures as well as its immigration and logistics coordination office remained intact.[57] Even more recently than that, it retained the ability not only to raise revenue but to move money.

Raising Money

Oil remained a revenue source long after the group lost control of major oil fields, along with extortion, kidnapping, and other criminal activity. A late-2018 U.S. government report noted extortion and taxation and the smuggling and sale of oil and oil products as the two main sources of the group's revenues.[58] Evidence for this emerges from military strike reports and media reports.

---

[55] Lead Inspector General for Overseas Contingency Operations, 2017b, p. 24.

[56] Lead Inspector General for Overseas Contingency Operations, 2017b, p. 24.

[57] UNSC, *Twenty-Second Report of the Analytical Support and Sanctions Monitoring Team Submitted Pursuant to Resolution 2368 (2017) Concerning ISIL (Da'esh), Al-Qaida and Associated Individuals and Entities*, S/2018/705, New York, July 27, 2018.

[58] U.S. Department of the Treasury, *National Terrorist Financing Risk Assessment*, Washington, D.C., 2018a, p. 7.

For example, regarding oil, the coalition reported in June 2018 the killing of four members of the Islamic State's oil and gas network during May 2018 operations in the central Euphrates River Valley in Syria.[59] A UNSC report issued in late July 2018 noted that the Islamic State had regained control of oil fields in northeastern Syria and continued to extract oil, both for its own use and for sale to locals.[60] As late as December 2018, the independent media outlet DeirezZor 24 was reporting that the Islamic State controlled oil fields in eastern Deir ez-Zor Governorate in Syria.[61]

The Islamic State continues to hold and move money. In December 2018, coalition strikes targeted "financial centers and capabilities" in Susah and As Shafah, Syria.[62] The ongoing campaign against such financial centers highlights one of the most important events of 2018 in signaling the financial future of the Islamic State.

From October 7, 2018, through October 9, 2018, Iraqi Special Operations Forces and the Kurdistan Region Counter Terrorism Forces, working with coalition forces, arrested ten members of what has become known as the Islamic State–linked al-Rawi financial network during operations in Baghdad and Erbil (we discuss the al-Rawi network later).[63] The arrest not only gave the opportunity for interrogation but also recovered documents about Islamic State finances.

The documents revealed an organization with substantial reserves and investments in numerous legitimate businesses. According to a report in the Iraqi media outlet Nas, citing the documents, the Islamic State has earned about $280 million from investments in real estate, fish farming, car dealing, and growing either marijuana or hashish near

---

59 CJTF-OIR PAO, "Coalition Kills Daesh Criminal Leader, Followers," press release, June 19, 2018a.

60 UNSC, 2018, p. 8.

61 "Daesh Makes Movements East of Deir Ezzor . . . And Controls Oil Wells in the Area," DeirezZor 24 website, December 28, 2018.

62 CJTF-OIR PAO, 2018c.

63 CJTF-OIR PAO, "Senior ISIS Facilitators Arrested in Iraq," press release, October 11, 2018b.

Baghdad.[64] Hotels have also been an investment target.[65] It was not clear whether the $280 million was net cash held in reserves or gross revenue, some of which had been spent. Nas reported that the total value invested by the Islamic State has been estimated at $250 million or $280 million.[66] An Iraqi expert on the Islamic State, Hisham al-Hashemi, quoted later in the article, estimated that the Islamic State drew $4 million monthly from its real estate investments in Baghdad alone.

Analysts had begun noting the shift in the Islamic State's revenue-generating methods by mid-2017.[67] By late 2018 and early 2019, there were various estimates of its assets. One estimate held that the Islamic State retained $400 million as it retreated from the cities it held through 2018.[68] The Nas article reported $250 million to $280 million. More recently, the United Nations noted that United Nations member states reported total Islamic State assets of $50 million to $300 million.[69]

Channeling that money into legitimate businesses is one way of preserving it and even increasing it. In some cases, the business owners might not have been aware of the sources of cash; in others, they may know and not care, eager for additional profits; or they might know and sympathize with the group's goals.[70] Aside from investing in businesses, the Islamic State is reported to have bulk cash storage sites.[71]

---

64 This paragraph is drawn from "Based in Karbala . . . Nas Discloses Details of the 'Al-Rawi Network' Implicated in Funding 'Daesh,'" Nas News (in Arabic), November 5, 2018.

65 Discussion with Kurdistan Regional Government security official, March 2019.

66 "Based in Karbala . . . ," 2018. Note that this figure is close to the reported earnings, so it is not clear whether earnings and investments are being conflated in the article.

67 Mansour and Al-Hashimi, 2017.

68 Warrick, 2018.

69 UNSC, *Eighth Report of the Secretary-General on the Threat Posed by ISIL (Da'esh) to International Peace and Security and the Range of United Nations Efforts in Support of Member States in Countering the Threat*, February 1, 2019.

70 Warrick, 2018; "Islamic State Has Been Stashing Millions of Dollars in Iraq and Abroad," *Economist*, February 22, 2018.

71 UNSC, 2019.

Media reports, citing the Kurdistan Regional Government, indicate that some of these assets are buried throughout Iraq and Syria and that raids have recovered gold bars and millions of dollars in cash.[72]

Reporting on the Islamic State's turn to illegal investment schemes and ownership of front companies is limited.[73] However, the activities reported indicate that it remains capable of engaging in sophisticated financial criminal activity to protect its existing war chest and to leverage it covertly to rebuild its organization.[74]

Moving Money

The Islamic State appears to be moving money using both informal financial institutions, such as those with which the al-Rawi network is involved, and couriers, meaning people hand-carrying the assets. In December 2016, the U.S. Department of the Treasury sanctioned Fawaz Muhammad Jubayr al-Rawi, described as a senior Islamic State financier; his company, the Hanifa Currency Exchange in Albu Kamal, Syria; and the Iraq-based Selselat al Thahab Money Exchange.[75] This was the first time Treasury had designated an Islamic State–linked money service business.[76] In June of the following year, Treasury sanctioned the Islamic State–linked Al-Kawthar Money Exchange and its owner, Umar al-Kubaysi, noting that "al-Kubaysi, as the owner of Al-Kawthar, reconciled deposits and withdrawals with the Hanifa Cur-

---

[72] "Daesh's Financing . . . Surprises of the Huge Criminal Network," 218 TV website (in Arabic), December 22, 2018.

[73] Romina McGuinness, "ISIS Net Worth REVEALED: Islamic State Is Worth £2.6BILLION Despite Losses," *Express*, April 26, 2018.

[74] In February, *Sky News Arabia* reported that the Iraqi National Intelligence Service had broken up a major financing network, arresting 15 Iraqis and 20 French citizens, and recovering $500 million ("Iraq Takes Daesh's Biggest Financiers by Surprise . . . and Seizes from Them 500 Million Dollars [العراق يباغت أكبر ممولي داعش.. ويحرمه من 500 مليون دولار]," *Sky News Arabia*, February 21, 2019). However, a conversation with a senior Iraqi official in the Prime Minister's office in March could not confirm this.

[75] U.S. Department of the Treasury, "Treasury Sanctions Senior ISIL Financier and Two Money Service Businesses," press release, Washington, D.C., December 13, 2016b.

[76] U.S. Department of the Treasury, "Treasury Sanctions Iraq-Based ISIS Financial Facilitation Network," press release, Washington, D.C., June 15, 2017.

rency Exchange," owned by al-Rawi. One day after the Al-Kawthar designation, on June 16, 2017, al-Rawi met an untimely end as the target of a coalition airstrike; the release about the strike noted that the coalition had previously killed three of his associates.[77] After that strike, the coalition was not finished with the al-Rawi network, as revealed by the October 2018 raid discussed earlier.

The Nas article cited earlier suggested that the ten people arrested were all senior officials of the U.S.-designated Selselat al Thahab Money Exchange, which the U.S. Department of the Treasury had sanctioned on the same day as Fawaz Muhammad Jubayr al-Rawi himself. The Nas report also noted that the al-Rawi network was linked to Iraqis running financial companies in Amman, Jordan, and that the network had transferred millions of dollars to support fighters and other activities throughout the Middle East and North Africa. The article also suggested that other members of the network had been arrested elsewhere, although those arrests had not been publicly announced.[78]

Other methods of moving money are available, according to our discussions with experts in Iraq in March 2019. Arrests of ISIS members have unveiled a network of more than 1,000 Islamic State fighters who smuggled an average of $25,000 per fighter from Syria into Iraq starting in September 2018, with security sources estimating a total amount of $200 million to be available in Iraq.[79] The February 2019 United Nations report also noted the smuggling of money into countries neighboring Iraq and Syria but did not describe how this smuggling took place.[80]

Conclusions on Islamic State Revenues

There have been two consistent patterns to Islamic State revenue raising. First has been an effort to raise money from local sources rather

77 CJTF-OIR PAO, 2017.

78 "Based in Karbala . . . ," 2018.

79 Discussion with Hisham al-Hashemi in Iraq, March 2019.

80 UNSC, 2019.

than relying on external donations. Second has been creative diversification. When it does not control territory, the group carries out what can be considered criminal activity, including extorting contracts, demanding protection money, and stealing and reselling goods, among other activities. When it does control territory, the group earned revenue from more–location-based activities, such as the sale of oil and gas from the fields it controls, from taxing and fining the local population, from selling antiquities, and from taxing transit, among other sources. We provide on-the-ground details of these efforts in Chapter Four. As of early 2019, one reported result of all these activities was the accumulation of substantial reserves.

But even without these reserves, the loss of the territorial caliphate will not necessarily mean the end of the Islamic State. Aside from creativity in revenue gathering, the group and its predecessors have also been able to control expenses, when necessary. We discuss Islamic State spending in Chapter Five.

CHAPTER FOUR

Raising Revenue: On-the-Ground View

When the Islamic State moved from working as a clandestine insurgency to an overt government, its interactions with people in Iraq and Syria multiplied. The many ways of raising revenue necessarily meant that residents in the territories it conquered had to deal with it on a regular basis. Over a wide range of territory, consistent accounts of the group's revenue-raising activities emerged. This chapter builds on Chapter Three, going further into depth in illustrating the Islamic State's revenue activities by drawing from direct evidence from residents of the so-called caliphate, supplemented by the analysis of experts with access to group documents or otherwise privileged information.

The Islamic State depended essentially on a diversity of revenue sources, including exploitation of natural resources, smuggling of antiquities, taxation, fees, and fines. In some cases, the collection of these revenue sources gave them in-depth knowledge of the people who lived in their territory, including the nature and location of their businesses and their livelihoods.

Methods

We conducted interviews with 16 people in the region who at one time or another lived under Islamic State rule. Three of these interviews were arranged with the help of al-Sharqiya 24, a small anti–Islamic

State activist group.[1] Our semistructured interview protocol included a combination of interview questions and broader discussion, enabling us to ask about topics that have been raised by analysts and researchers throughout the lifetime of the Islamic State and its predecessors but also enabling people to raise issues that only those with firsthand knowledge and experience would be aware of. All interviews were conducted in spring 2017, when the Islamic State was under tremendous military pressure but before it had been defeated in Raqqa, elsewhere in Syria, and in selected locations in Iraq. Thus, we were able to interview people who had previously lived under Islamic State rule and people who were still living under Islamic State rule. Experts consulted included Aymenn Jawad al-Tamimi of the Middle East Forum; Jalal al-Hamad, director of the Justice for Life Organization based in Deir ez-Zor; Fadel Abu Ragheef, an expert on radical organizations, based in Baghdad; and Hisham al-Hashemi, of the Al-Nahrain Centre for Strategic Studies in Baghdad.

Unfortunately, we have no way to confirm the information shared by the residents living under Islamic State rule. However, we judged the veracity based on our long experience working on the Islamic State and its predecessors (some members of the research team have been working on the group, using its own documents, since early 2007), media reports, and government and multilateral organization reports. Admittedly, there is always a chance this information is incorrect.

For purposes of reporting the results of the interviews, we assigned each respondent a designator of a number or number and letter combination, with the correspondence between the designator and the respondent known only to one of the project team. Statements are attributed by respondent designator with any identifying information, for the most part other than the person's former location under Islamic State rule, minimized. For monetary values, we opted to leave these values largely in the currencies mentioned in the interview reports, but one rule of thumb is that one U.S. dollar was equal to 500 Syrian

---

[1] Al-Sharqiya 24 is the group of which a man with the pseudonym Samer was a member. Samer is the author, along with editor Mike Thompson and illustrator Scott Coelho, of *The Raqqa Diaries: Escape from the Islamic State*, Interlink Pub Group, 2017.

pounds and 1,260 Iraqi dinars at the time of the interviews.[2] Accordingly, when the interview reports give values in Syrian pounds or Iraqi dinars, we also include dollar amounts calculated at these exchange rates.[3] Note that the interviews leave open numerous questions, such as why certain fees were different in Iraq and Syria. Given the small sample and the lack of comprehensive data, we are reluctant to draw definitive conclusions about a variety of Islamic State policies. However, the interviews provide solid evidence regarding the broad outlines of Islamic State revenue-raising activities.

Resource Revenue Sources

We start with a brief account of resource extraction. This includes revenue from oil and the oil supply chain and antiquities. We then move to nonoil forms of revenue. These include taxes on the population, transit-related taxes, municipal fees, agricultural fees, fines and punishments, and confiscation. Unless otherwise specified, all information in the following subsections is from interview subjects.

Oil and the Oil Supply Chain

Residents living under Islamic State rule reported a variety of prices for hydrocarbons and had differing understandings about how and where the group sold oil. We start with reports from the oil-rich Deir ez-Zor Governorate, including Deir ez-Zor city, Mayadin, and Albu Kamal. There, residents reported that the Islamic State used transportable oil stations and sold oil for anywhere between \$25 and \$75 per barrel.[4]

---

[2] For Iraqi dinars, the exchange rate is the average of the monthly market rates from January 2017 through June 2017 (Central Bank of Iraq, "Price Indicators, Exchange Rate, Market Price" online data, 2019). The exact figure was 1,261.17. Determining the Syrian rate is much harder because there was an official rate and a much more depreciated market, or black-market, rate. The black-market rate had been about 440 Syrian pounds to the dollar in January 2016 but depreciated to more than 500 in March of that year (Mike Bird, "The Syrian Pound's Black Market Moves Are a Futures Contract on Bashar Al Assad," *Wall Street Journal*, April 1, 2016). We do not have similar reports from 2017.

[3] Note that in some cases, we round to nearest whole-dollar amounts.

[4] Respondents 1 and 2.

Sales were not only within Islamic State territory but were also made through traders to the Bashar al-Assad regime and liberated areas in Syria, Kurdish areas, and even Iraq.[5] One resident reported that, at one point, oil was sent via pipeline to a regime refinery in Homs.[6] Another resident reported that the Islamic State recruited technical experts to help it maintain the fields and extract oil.[7] The group apparently also tried to limit its financial risk after Operation Tidal Wave II started. One resident reported that it started licensing the operation of certain wells for large amounts of money, with the monthly figure of 150 million Syrian pounds (about $300,000) mentioned. One such person participating was allegedly Fawaz al-Rawi, identified by the United States as a major Islamic State financier.[8] Coalition forces killed him in an airstrike in June 2017.[9]

Aleppo did not produce its own oil, and one resident reported that they were receiving oil from Kurdish regions of Syria.[10] The U.S.-partnered SDF, dominated by the Kurdish People's Protective Units (Yekîneyên Parastina Gel [YPG] in Kurdish) led the battle to liberate Raqqa, the Islamic State's reported capital, in 2017. Residents of Islamic State–ruled Mosul reported receiving oil originating in Syria.[11] But the Islamic State also controlled the Qayarah oil field in Iraq and produced low-quality oil there for use in Mosul.[12] One Mosul resident who worked in the oil sector also said that the Islamic State sold oil to Turkey.[13]

---

[5] Respondents 4a and 4b.

[6] Respondent 4c.

[7] Respondent 5.

[8] Respondent 5; U.S. Department of the Treasury, 2016b.

[9] CJTF-OIR PAO, 2017.

[10] Respondents 3a and 3b.

[11] Respondents 6, 7, and 10.

[12] Respondents 8, 9, and 10.

[13] Respondent 10.

Antiquities

The Islamic State classified antiquities as a resource, managed under its Ministry of Natural Resources [Diwan Rikaz].[14] One method the group used to exploit antiquities was to license people to find, excavate, and sell them, then to take a portion of the sale.[15] One person formerly in Deir ez-Zor said that the Islamic State's Ministry of Natural Resources licensed people to participate in the antiquities trade and then collected 20 percent of their revenues.[16] But at other times, the Islamic State appeared to participate directly in the trade. In one case, the group brought in heavy machinery to excavate in Salihiya, a town 30 km from Albu Kamal, Syria, as well as in Marea, another region close to Albu Kamal.[17] This respondent noted that most of the antiquities were small items, although one was a gold bracelet from the Babylonian era, sold to traffickers for 200 million Syrian pounds, or about $400,000. He and two others said most of the smuggled antiquities were sold in Syria and Turkey.[18] One respondent from Mosul said antiquities, such as those looted from the Mosul museum, were sent first to Syria en route to Turkey.[19]

Nonresource Revenue Sources

As noted in Chapter Three, although the Islamic State may have been best known for its oil-related activities, it actually had a diversified nonoil revenue stream. Well into the success of Operation Tidal Wave II, this nonoil revenue stream may have been larger than the oil revenue stream. In late spring 2016, the United States estimated that

---

[14] Andrew Keller, "Documenting ISIL's Antiquities Trafficking: The Looting and Destruction of Iraqi and Syrian Cultural Heritage: What We Know and What Can be Done," remarks at the Metropolitan Museum of Art, New York, September 29, 2015.

[15] Keller, 2015.

[16] Respondent 12.

[17] Respondent 5.

[18] Respondents 5, 9, and 10.

[19] Respondent 9.

annual revenues from taxation amounted to $360 million, whereas annual oil revenues had been cut to about $250 million.[20] The high levels of taxation were enabled by control of millions of people in the Islamic State's territory.

For purposes of the Islamic State's continued longevity, parts of the nonoil revenue stream are actually more dangerous than its exploitation of oil. Oil revenues depended in large part on territorial control. However, taxation depended on collecting data about the financial and commercial activities of the residents within its territory. Given its record-keeping practices, it is likely that the Islamic State still has vast amounts of information about the people it formerly ruled. In the next sections, we discuss taxation, fees, fines and punishments, and confiscations.

Taxes

The Islamic State ruled a territory and acted as a government, dispensing its own form of justice. Part of acting as a government included levying a variety of taxes and fees. In this section, we discuss taxes. Taxes included collections based on property, revenue, farming output, and levies related to transit. Their collection appeared to be highly structured and organized. In addition, a variety of Islamic State ministries or departments were involved, including Economic Security [Amn Iqtissadi], the Zakat Ministry, and the Agricultural Ministry.

Notably, the taxes the Islamic State charged conformed with taxes required by or mentioned in Islamic law. Attempts to conform with Islamic law may have reflected the Islamic State's view that it was restoring the historic caliphate. But this also could have been a messaging strategy, meant to convince others, particularly observant Muslims, that it was a true Muslim organization. Alternatively, rates and requirements could have been such that the Islamic State saw application of Islamic law as a way to collect large amounts of revenue—an instrumental use of Islamic law and nothing more.

---

[20] Torbati, 2016.

Taxes on Property, Revenue, and Farming Output

Islamic law defines a tax, known as *zakah*, or *zakat*, under which Muslims are required to give 2.5 percent of their net worth each year; this is one of the five pillars of Islam.[21] Most of the respondents indicated that the Islamic State collected a 2.5 percent tax; this was true in Deir ez-Zor Governorate,[22] rural Aleppo,[23] and Mosul.[24] In at least one case in Mosul, the reported tax on a salary was 5 percent.[25]

One respondent from Deir ez-Zor said that each person living in the city had to go to the Zakat Bureau to inform the Islamic State of their properties so that the Islamic State could calculate tax due. Income was recorded in registers. Furthermore, the committee inspected people's property, and failing to report resulted in double the payment.[26] This took place in Mosul as well: One respondent said residents had to declare assets, including property, businesses, and jewelry.[27] In the case of Mosul, cheating could result in jail. Collections by the Islamic State were generally annual, although, in the case of high-income individuals, the Islamic State would collect biannually or even monthly, according to one respondent from Mayadin in Deir ez-Zor Governorate.

The Islamic State also imposed taxes on money transfers, both in Syria, on Syrian workers transferring money to their families back home, and in Iraq, on salary transfers for government employees. In Syria, according to a former resident of rural Aleppo, the Islamic State had started forcing people to pay a currency charge of 5,000 Syrian pounds ($10), and an additional $50 for the $300 her husband transferred every month from Lebanon.[28] In Mosul, the relative of a retired member of the Iraqi armed forces reported that the Islamic State taxed

---

21 "Zakah," in Esposito, 2003.

22 Respondents 1, 2, 4a, 4c, 5, and 12.

23 Respondent 3a.

24 Respondents 7, 8, 10, and 11.

25 Respondent 9.

26 Respondents 4a and 4c.

27 Respondent 11.

28 Respondent 3a.

the former government employee about 7 percent of the $700 he received every two months.[29] Another retired member of the armed forces in Mosul indicated that these transfer taxes were progressive, with the rate up to 15 percent for amounts of more than $700.[30]

Taxes extended to businesses. For example, the Islamic State applied the 2.5 percent rate discussed earlier to businesses as well.[31] Although 2.5 percent was the usual rate, it could vary. One resident of Deir ez-Zor city reported that he paid a rate of 3 percent on the stock in his business.[32] As with personal taxes, the Islamic State inspected businesses, reviewing invoices and sale and purchase records, often doing so unannounced.[33] In Mosul, one resident noted that, in the case of bakeries, the group would send inspectors to check the quantity of wheat held in stock and then estimate production value, which would then be taxed.[34] In addition, results were recorded, according to another Deir ez-Zor resident: The revenues of large companies and corporate owners were audited and recorded in special registers; sales, purchases, audited capital, and profits had to be registered as well.[35] Taxation was levied not only on operations but at the start of a business, with a 2.5 percent tax on capital as part of gaining an Islamic State license when opening a business.[36]

The Islamic State's taxes also extended to agriculture. Islamic law has a number of taxes pertaining to agriculture. First, zakat applies to agricultural produce.[37] But in some periods of Islamic history, there has also been a tax called *ushr*, or the tithe or tenth, which was a tax levied

---

[29] Respondent 6.

[30] Respondent 9.

[31] Respondent 4b.

[32] Respondent 1.

[33] Respondent 4c.

[34] Respondent 10.

[35] Respondent 4a.

[36] Respondent 12.

[37] "Zakah," in Esposito, 2003.

on the produce of agricultural land.[38] This apparently was not meant to be always 10 percent. Some sources indicate that the tax was to be 10 percent on produce stemming from land that was watered naturally, such as by rain or rivers, and 5 percent was to be levied on produce stemming from land that was irrigated by physical effort, such as with a bucket and well-drawn water.[39]

Agricultural taxation was handled by the Islamic State's Agriculture Ministry, which also managed sales, at least of wheat and grains in Deir ez-Zor.[40] In some ways, this duplicated the role previously played by the Syrian Farmers Union, such as in its management of land and irrigation.[41] In addition, the Islamic State would prevent farmers in Deir ez-Zor Governorate from harvesting their wheat without permission; farmers had to show proof of zakat payment.[42] Management was not always efficient or production-maximizing: One respondent from Albu Kamal reported that fertilizers were scarce because the Islamic State needed them for explosives.[43]

Respondents reported the Islamic State taxing agricultural land.[44] In accordance with the tax called *ushr*, the Islamic State reportedly taxed the value of wheat and grains at 10 percent. Respondents in both Deir ez-Zor Governorate and rural Aleppo reported agricultural produce taxes of 5 percent and 10 percent, depending on the type of produce and whether the land is irrigated.[45] However, at least in one case, it

---

38 "Ushr," in Esposito, 2003.

39 Abdul-Qadeem Zalloom, *Funds in the Khilafah State: Al-Amwal fi Dowlat Al-Khilafah*, 2nd ed., London: Al-Khilafah Publications, May 1988.

40 Respondent 4a.

41 Respondent 4c.

42 Respondents 3b, 4b, and 6.

43 Respondent 5.

44 Respondent 2.

45 Respondents 3a and 6.

taxed cotton at 2.5 percent of the value.[46] Some respondents indicated that the Islamic State sometimes took payment of the tax in kind.[47]

Transit-Related Taxes

During its territorial rule in Syria, the Islamic State controlled roads that linked much of the rest of Syria, particularly the Kurdish area in the northeast and regime-held territory in the west. Trade continued, and the Islamic State profited from charging transit taxes—in at least one case, a figure of $1,000 for a truck carrying 28 tons of produce was cited.[48] In addition, Islamic State–held regions traded with other regions, providing additional transit-related fees.

Respondents reported a variety of ways that the Islamic State profited from transit. For example, respondents in Deir ez-Zor said that a relative with a truck paid taxes on the value of the merchandise he transported into Islamic State territory and outside; this was reported to be at the 2.5 percent rate.[49] Money was collected at checkpoints with no apparent right of appeal; at least one person expressed doubt as to whether the money taken at checkpoints was given to the group or kept by the checkpoint guards.[50] But as with most Islamic State activities, this involved a formal bureaucracy and procedures. Another respondent from Deir ez-Zor reported that goods were subject to invoice inspection with taxes assessed on the value. The Islamic State inspected freight forwarding offices and required these offices to submit statements on outgoing and incoming trucks and the types of goods they were carrying. Furthermore, outgoing trucks had to obtain an authorization by the Islamic State, and each truck driver who obtained an authorization could be accompanied by one person only.[51]

---

46 Respondent 5.

47 For example, Respondent 6.

48 Raja Abdulrahim, "In Syria's Mangled Economy, Truckers Stitch Together Warring Regions," *Wall Street Journal*, May 24, 2016.

49 Respondents 2 and 12.

50 Respondent 4c.

51 Respondent 4a.

These reports were consistent across Islamic State locations. In rural Aleppo, trucks had to pay fees upon entry and exit, whether they were empty or full.[52] In Mosul, one respondent reported that the Islamic State taxed trucks going into and out of the area at $100 per ton.[53] Another noted that both trucks and cars exiting and entering the Islamic State's Mosul territory were taxed.[54] This entry tax also apparently affected the final market price of goods in Mosul.[55]

It remains unclear what amounts were raised by the Islamic State on transit because taxes reported varied greatly from one respondent to another. As an example, Iraqi expert Fadel Abu Ragheef believed that the Islamic State imposed a tax of $600 to $800 on every truck transporting oil, while most respondents reported that trucks had to pay a tax of $100 to $200 per ton transported; Iraqi expert Hisham al-Hashemi gave his estimation as $100 per ton. Other respondents nonetheless underscored that taxes on transit were generally calculated on the basis of the 2.5 percent zakat applied to the value of the merchandise transported.

Municipal Fees

In its role as governing authority, the Islamic State charged a variety of fees. In Syria, the Islamic State imposed fees for services it obtained for free that were actually provided by the regime, such as water and electricity.[56] It also added a flurry of fees for other services, such as municipal cleaning and rental of public market space. Despite these fees, as we discuss at the end of this subsection, the reported level of service provision was quite low.

---

[52] Respondent 3a.

[53] Respondent 9.

[54] Respondent 10.

[55] Respondent 11.

[56] Other reports confirm that electricity had been provided by the Syrian government. This appeared to be common in gas-fired generating plants in Islamic State territory, for which the Syrian government paid salaries, supplied spare parts, and received some of the electricity, sending the rest to the grid in Islamic State lands (Erika Solomon, "The ISIS Economy: Meet the New Boss," *Financial Times*, January 5, 2015; Erika Solomon and Ahmed Mhidi, "ISIS Inc.: Syria's 'Mafia-Style' Gas Deals with Jihadis," *Financial Times*, October 15, 2015).

Fees for Services in Cities and Towns

Reports of rates paid varied by area, but respondents from all areas reported paying a variety of fees. Respondents from Deir ez-Zor city and Albu Kamal reported fees for electricity and municipal cleaning.[57] Amounts in and near Deir ez-Zor city were reported as 1,000 Syrian pounds (about $2) for 1 amp of electricity from Islamic State generators; 1,000 Syrian pounds ($2) monthly for water; 500 Syrian pounds ($1) monthly for city cleaning fees; 20,000 Syrian pounds ($40) to renew an identification card; and other amounts for using medical clinics, previously free under the Syrian regime.[58] Another respondent from rural Deir ez-Zor also reported municipal and water fees as 1,000 Syrian pounds ($2) every month, but paid every two months.[59] Later in Islamic State rule in Deir ez-Zor, after it had started issuing its own currency, it charged 1.5 Islamic State dirhams for each telephone line.[60] A respondent from Mayadin reported this as a monthly fee of 2.25 dirhams, to be paid at the post office.[61] One report put the value of Islamic State silver dirham at about $1.[62]

Beyond personal fees, there were business fees. The Islamic State authorized bakery operations to the highest bidders, who then paid an annual lease.[63] Taxis paid a yearly tax of 45,000 Syrian pounds ($90).[64] And in at least one market, traders rented a space for about $50 monthly.[65]

One respondent from Albu Kamal reported a detailed menu of fees, including 500 Syrian pounds ($1) for a landline; 3,500 Syrian

---

[57] Respondents 1 and 4b.

[58] Respondents 1 and 2.

[59] Respondent 12.

[60] Respondent 4a.

[61] Respondent 4c.

[62] Lizzie Dearden, "ISIS Claims to Mint Gold and Silver Coins for Currency Free from 'Satanic' Global Economy," *Independent*, June 24, 2015.

[63] Respondent 4a.

[64] Respondent 5.

[65] Respondent 5.

pounds ($7) each for water and electricity; 500 Syrian pounds ($1) for cleaning taxes; 15,000 Syrian pounds ($30) yearly for a motorcycle driver's license; 30,000 Syrian pounds ($60) for an automobile driver's license; a per-passenger fee to taxi drivers starting at 400 Syrian pounds (80 cents) and depending on distance; and an annual taxi fee of between $80 and $100. In addition, the Islamic State charged fees at medical clinics, including $150 for a caesarean-section birth.[66]

Some rates appeared to be higher in rural Aleppo. One resident reported water and electricity fees of 4,000 Syrian pounds ($8) per month.[67] Another confirmed this, reporting 2,000 Syrian pounds ($4) for water and 2,000 Syrian pounds ($4) for electricity, in contrast to the 500 Syrian pounds ($1) the Syrian regime used to charge. This person added that the charge for a telephone landline was 6,000 Syrian pounds ($12), and the charge to renew an identification card, which apparently had to be done in Raqqa, was 5,000 to 10,000 Syrian pounds (or $10 to $20).[68]

Rates were higher still in Mosul, Iraq. The monthly water charge was reported to be about $25, and municipal fees amounted to $6.[69] Other respondents reported weekly fees of 2,000 Iraqi dinars ($1.60) each for security and street cleaning, and 5,000 Iraqi dinars ($4) weekly for water.[70] Bakeries reportedly had to pay a tax of 5,000 Iraqi dinars ($4) if they used a generator.[71] Other respondents provided somewhat different numbers but still higher than those in Syria. One respondent reported monthly charges of $4 each on water, electricity, and municipality fees, with stores paying the equivalent of $10. In addition, the Islamic State charged $100 for a new, required Islamic State license plate.[72] Another person reported the license-plate fee as about $40 to

---

66 Respondent 5.

67 Respondent 3a.

68 Respondent 3b.

69 Respondent 6.

70 Respondent 8.

71 Respondent 10.

72 Respondent 9.

$50.[73] Initially, the Islamic State talked of having people change their identity cards to Islamic State identity cards for 10,000 Iraqi dinars ($8), but this appears not to have been implemented, and people continued using their Iraqi identification cards.[74] However, the renewal of a lost identity card or the issuance of a new one for a newborn cost the equivalent of $10, about the same as in Syria.[75]

Agricultural Fees

The Islamic State applied fees to agriculture as well and made money from renting agricultural land. In one case, the Islamic State confiscated government agricultural land and rented it for 5,000 Syrian pounds ($10) per year plus a percentage of output (as described earlier); the group also confiscated cattle and then rented them to farmers or gave them away.[76] Another respondent reported similar amounts: rent ranging from 500 Syrian pounds ($1) to 2,000 Syrian pounds ($4) per dunam per year, depending on location and whether it was irrigated.[77] A *dunam* is a measure of land area, used in parts of the former Ottoman Empire and equal to about 900 square meters or about one quarter of an acre.[78] In rural Aleppo, the group expropriated a local landlord and rented his land to local farms at 10,000 Syrian pounds ($20) per hectare; the group also charged 12,000 Syrian pounds ($24) for annual irrigation fees.[79]

Did the Islamic State Actually Provide Services for Fees?

Although the Islamic State did indeed govern a large portion of the territory of Iraq and Syria, turning it into a temporary territorial caliphate, the organization provided only modest services. Some accounts said the provision of services occurred toward the beginning of the

---

[73] Respondent 10.

[74] Respondent 10.

[75] Respondent 6.

[76] Respondent 2.

[77] Respondent 12.

[78] "Dunam," Oxford Living Dictionaries website, 2019.

[79] Respondent 3b.

group's rule. Near Deir ez-Zor city, for example, the group initially helped widows and orphans and distributed some free medicines.[80] In Deir ez-Zor city, it fixed some of the main roads and installed lighting but paved with dirt rather than asphalt. The group even took complaints via a form.[81] Elsewhere in Deir ez-Zor Governorate and Raqqa, the group cleaned streets, paved roads, restored traffic lights, and built sidewalks and markets, sometimes employing civilians.[82]

But for the most part, people reported that service provision declined as the Islamic State's rule waned. In Deir ez-Zor, respondents reported that the Islamic State did very little to fix roads or subsidize staples and cited only one case of the distribution of subsidized bread.[83] When the Islamic State did fix roads, it spent very little.[84]

Accounts were similar in other locations: modest services but not at the level the Syrian regime provided. In rural Aleppo, the Islamic State would reconnect water and electricity after bombings but do little else. Unsubsidized, the price of bread rose. However, the group did provide charity to very poor people after inspecting their living conditions.[85] Another person in rural Aleppo reported no Islamic State expenditures on street cleaning, fixing roads, or subsidizing bread and other staples.[86]

Mosul appeared to be a particularly high-service area, at least at first. Initially, the Islamic State provided streetlights, fixed roads, put up decorations, cleaned and organized the old market, and opened a garden with games (charging a fee to enter).[87] Opinions about subsidizing bread and staples differed, with some saying the Islamic State did so initially; others saying it did so only for supporters; and still others

---

[80] Respondent 2.

[81] Respondent 4a.

[82] Respondents 4b, 4c, and 5.

[83] Respondents 1, 2, and 4c.

[84] Respondent 4b.

[85] Respondent 3a.

[86] Respondent 3b.

[87] Respondents 6, 7, 8, 9, 10, and 11.

saying it did not do so at all.[88] One person noted that, eventually, the group even banned the distribution of the Iraqi food ration, a nationwide, free-food package distribution that had begun under the reign of Saddam Hussein.[89] Possible reasons for doing so included using the food for the group's own personnel or selling it to raise revenue. Notably, this respondent's statement suggests that the national government distributed the food ration even in Islamic State territory.[90]

Only one person said there was distribution of free food and medicine but very little, only initially, and mostly to supporters.[91] The Islamic State also tried to keep other government services running, with one person reporting that teachers were forced to work for free and under threat of death if they did not fulfill the Islamic State's orders.[92]

Fines and Punishments

The Islamic State also gained revenues from administering its own form of justice. This involved enforcement of its interpretation of Islamic law but also involved such mundane violations as driving infractions.

Among the first class, fines were commonly imposed on women for wearing "un-Islamic" clothing, for example not wearing a *niqab*—a veil that leaves only the area around the eyes clear—or a *khimar*—

---

[88] Respondents 6, 7, 9, and 11.

[89] Respondent 11.

[90] Other sources are conflicting on this. A report dating from August 2014 noted that the food ration system, known as the Public Distribution System, had "broken down in militant-held areas" (Maggie Fick and Maha El Dahan, "Exclusive: Islamic State Militants Grab New Weapon—Iraqi Wheat," Reuters, August 13, 2014). However, a later report from the International Monetary Fund suggested at least some Public Distribution System goods were still being provided in Islamic State areas: "The intensification of the conflict with ISIS has negatively affected the coverage of the distribution system, impacting the disbursement of some products to eligible households in areas under ISIS control. ISIS' smuggling and abuse of the system has also been reported" (Amgad Hegazy, "Food and Electricity Subsidies in Iraq," in Koba Gvenetadze and Amgad Hegazy, *Iraq: Selected Issues*, Washington, D.C.: International Monetary Fund, Country Report No. 15/236, August 2015, p. 17).

[91] Respondent 9.

[92] Respondent 8.

a transparent fabric that covers the face—or wearing a colorful rather than black *abaya*—a head-to-toe robe that covers the entire body. Fines were also placed on men who did not conform to the group's rules of Islamic appearance, such as by having no beard or wearing pants that were too long, rather than short in the style of the Pakistani *shalwar kameez*.

In Deir ez-Zor Governorate, the fine for wearing the niqab improperly varied from 2,500 Syrian pounds to 8,000 Syrian pounds ($5 to $16), with higher fines and jail for no niqab and higher fines of up to 20,000 Syrian pounds ($40) for other forms of un-Islamic dress.[93] But even with a niqab, there was a fine of 200 Syrian pounds (80 cents) if the woman was not also wearing a veil, and 1,000 Syrian pounds ($2) if a woman was not covering her hands with gloves.[94] Furthermore, the Islamic State opened stores for Islamic clothing and forced people who committed infractions to buy from them.[95]

The Islamic State appeared to be less strict in rural Aleppo. There, a woman wearing un-Islamic clothing would have to buy the right clothing for about $14, but it is not clear that she would be fined as well. However, tying up one's hair with a hair clip under the niqab could merit a fine of 12,000 Syrian pounds, or about $24; women in the religious police [*Hisba*], would do the searching.[96] For men in rural Aleppo, the Islamic State would cut the ends off pants legs if they were too long. Some men opted to fold their pants up but were fined 2,000 Syrian pounds ($4) for each fold.[97]

As with fees, rates appeared to be much higher in Mosul for violations pertaining to Islamic dress. In addition, people mentioned whipping more often. Classes in Islamic law were also sometimes required.[98] In Mosul, a woman wearing kohl (eyeliner) or not wearing the niqab

---

[93] Respondents 1, 2, 5, and 12.

[94] Respondent 1.

[95] Respondent 5.

[96] Respondent 3a.

[97] Respondent 3b.

[98] Respondent 11.

properly would be fined between $4 and $40, and either she or her husband could be whipped.[99] An improperly trimmed beard could result in a 25,000 Iraqi dinar fine, about $20. Multiple infractions could result in a $100 fine and time in prison.[100] Men's pants were also an issue: Pants that were too tight could bring about a 25,000 Iraqi dinar fine ($20).[101]

Smoking, which has been declared contrary to Islamic law, merited high fines. In the area of Deir ez-Zor, someone caught smoking would be jailed and pressed to name the seller, but $100 could be exchanged for freedom. When caught, the seller would be fined from $3,000 to upwards of $30,000, with two people reporting that the fine was five times the value of the merchandise.[102] In rural Aleppo, cigarette traders were fined one gram of gold for every ten cigarette packs.[103] However, in Mosul, it appeared that the fines were lower. Smokers were fined 15,000 Iraqi dinars ($12) and received 30 lashes.[104] Cigarette traders could be fined a minimum of $200 but up to $1,700 for $10,000 worth of merchandise and imprisoned for six months.[105]

Alongside these fines for violations of Islamic law were fines for traffic violations, ranging from $4 to about $21.[106] In Mosul, one resident was fined 25,000 Iraqi dinars ($20) for a motorcycle infraction.[107]

There were also penalties for smuggling people. Human smugglers who specialized in moving people out of Islamic State territory would be hanged if caught but could sometimes buy their way out of a death sentence for $10,000.[108] Notably, numerous respondents from

---

99 Respondents 6, 7, and 9.

100 Respondent 6.

101 Respondent 9.

102 Respondents 2, 5, and 12.

103 Respondent 3b.

104 Respondent 10.

105 Respondents 7 and 10.

106 Respondent 10.

107 Respondent 7.

108 Respondents 2 and 4c.

a variety of locations said that it also appeared that the group collaborated with human smugglers and took a cut of the smuggling fee.[109]

Confiscation

One of the generally underreported income streams is that resulting from confiscation. The Islamic State earned significant revenue just by taking things. There are two forms of confiscation within Islamic law as applied by the Islamic State, and these are often conflated. The first is spoils [*ghanima*], or goods taken in war.[110] The second is booty [*fay'*], or goods taken from adversaries but not in the action of war.[111] As described later, the Islamic State's confiscation operations targeted not only individuals but entire factories, which were then stripped down and sold. Note that, although we present Syria first in earlier sections, we start with Mosul here because that is where confiscations appeared to be the largest.

The Islamic State's most well-known confiscations were of the money in banks in cities it conquered, as described in Chapter Three. The Iraqi government estimated that the Islamic State captured about $830 million in Iraq alone.[112]

But on a personal level, confiscations hit people who were not Sunni Muslims particularly hard. In Deir ez-Zor, Syria, Christians reportedly fled before the Islamic State took control, and the group confiscated their properties and gave them to its members.[113] In Iraq, all respondents in the Mosul area underlined the systematic confiscation of assets owned by Christians and other minorities, the highest prevalence being in the city of Mosul, which was home to a large

---

[109] Respondents 2, 3a, 6, 9, and 10.

[110] Aaron Y. Zelin, "The Clairvoyant: Boko Haram's Media and The Islamic State Connection?" *Jihadology*, January 27, 2015a; Aaron Y. Zelin, "Between the Islamic State and al-Qaeda in Tunisia," Washington Institute for Near East Policy, May 11, 2015b.

[111] Bernard Lewis, *From Babel to Dragomans: Interpreting the Middle East*, New York: Oxford University Press, 2004, p. 61.

[112] Jack Moore, "ISIS Members Plundered $800 Million from Iraq, Central Bank Says," *Newsweek*, August 9, 2017.

[113] Respondents 4a and 5.

number of Shia and Christian people, among many other groups. Initially, the Islamic State demanded of the Christians the *jizya*, an Islamic tax on tolerated minorities. However, most Christians refused and left the city, and the Islamic State then confiscated their property, including stopping them on their way out, searching them, and stripping them of belongings. Women of the religious police searched exiting women for jewelry. Some of these belongings were sold to others remaining in the city, or given to the Islamic State's followers, and the Islamic State would rent or give away the property.[114]

Mosul residents also consistently reported that the Islamic State confiscated factories and businesses owned by big companies or fleeing residents. At first, the group tried to run the companies and, in some cases, succeeded because it could hire experts with a wide range of skills.[115] But, in many cases, the group failed and then dismantled the plants and sold the equipment, reportedly shipping it across the border and selling it in Syrian regime areas.[116] Beyond factory confiscations, respondents said the Islamic State stole from hospitals, clinics, and gyms; dismantled pipelines and an electrical plant; and even stole the metal benches on the main streets of Mosul and solar panels for sale in Syrian regime areas.[117] Outside the city, the group confiscated farms owned by Shias and sold the farm animals to Syria.[118] Without identifying the owners of the farms, another respondent noted that farm animals were confiscated and shipped to Syria.[119]

Confiscations also took place in Syria. The Islamic State confiscated businesses in Deir ez-Zor and even dismantled part of the train tracks and sold the metal. It also confiscated cattle, as well as houses,

---

[114] Respondents 6, 7, 8, 9, 10, and 11.

[115] Respondent 11.

[116] Respondents 6, 7, 8, 9, and 11.

[117] Respondents 7 and 9.

[118] Respondent 7. We do not have further information as to whether these were sold in Syrian regime areas or Islamic State areas, or to whom they were sold.

[119] Respondent 8.

either renting them or giving them away, as it did in Mosul.[120] In some cases, the Islamic State targeted smaller companies; in one example, it took over a palm tree farm and sold the trees to Jordanian smugglers.[121] Seizures apparently extended to money. In Deir ez-Zor, one respondent reported that the group would fabricate accusations and violations as a pretext for collecting money from wealthy people.[122]

Conclusion

In this chapter and Chapter Three, we showed that the Islamic State had a diversified revenue stream. Although perhaps best known for bank looting and oil sales, its revenue-raising activities reached far beyond these two activities. Drawing on Islamic law and its control of territory, the group also collected personal and business taxes, charged fees for various services, and collected fines for violations of religious strictures and civil violations, such as traffic violations.

Most perniciously, the Islamic State appeared to collect records on the individuals over which it ruled. Previous research has shown that the group kept numerous records on a variety of topics.[123] These involved its personnel rosters, revenue sources, and expenditures, along with doctrine and strategy manuals. Our interviews with people who lived in Islamic State territory and were exposed to the group indicate that the group also developed extensive records on nonmembers, specifically on their assets and business activities. The group also kept records on political, tribal, and sectarian loyalties to inform decisions about whom to target for taxation and extortion and what methods to use. With the Islamic State now pushed out of its territorial holdings, there is no reason to think it has abandoned or destroyed the extensive records it developed on the Syrians and Iraqis who lived under its rule.

---

120 Respondent 2.

121 Respondent 5.

122 Respondent 4a.

123 Johnston et al., 2016.

CHAPTER FIVE

Islamic State Expenditures

One of the great advantages of destroying the Islamic State's territorial caliphate is that it reduced the group's revenue-producing opportunities. Taking back oil and gas fields reduced the revenue it gained from sale of these resources. Liberating population centers reduced the group's ability to gain revenue from the population—from taxing them, fining them for violating Islamic State rules, or charging them fees for services. Taking back territory also reduced the group's ability to excavate and sell antiquities.

With the goal of trying to reestablish the caliphate, the Islamic State still needs money to fund its activities. The Islamic State spends its money in ways similar to those of other terrorist and insurgent groups. Some of its money goes to paying its fighters' salaries; some goes to weapon procurement; and, when it controlled territory, some was earmarked for maintaining the vast infrastructure of its caliphate and the provision of basic services for those living within that territory. Now that it no longer controls territory, the Islamic State is spending considerably less on governing and providing services.

At the Islamic State's peak, running a caliphate and waging jihad required the group to incur substantial costs to pay for the implementation and sustainment of its governing policies, religious policing, salaries for its military personnel, war materiel, its vast media operations, and many other varied activities that helped provide the group with legitimacy. Since the group's inception in the early 2000s, its internal financial documents suggest that it has managed to maintain a demanding accounting system to avoid fatal budget deficits and having to seek large amounts of external financing through donations to keep the movement alive. This system also helped trace corruption among members, which both occurred and was a concern to the group.[1]

In this chapter, we examine the Islamic State's expenditure profile: the types of goods and services on which it spends its money and the share of the budget it typically allocates to each category of expenditure. This is the basis for a sketch of the group's potential future expenditure profile and discussion of the implications of its spending practices for its medium- to long-term financial sustainability. Some of our conclusions are based on evidence from the group's behavior in situations that approximated its status as an insurgency with state-building ambitions, such as in Anbar Governorate in 2005 and 2006, but we also look at leaner years, in which the group held little territory, such as in Mosul in 2008 and 2009, a closer approximation to its state in 2019. We draw on these earlier periods and evidence from recent expenditures to compare the size and composition of Islamic State expenditures and assess what these patterns likely mean for its near- and medium-term future strategy and sustainability.

Some analysts have argued that costs associated with the Islamic State's ambition of maintaining a territorial caliphate would be too large for the group to cover.[2] Over time, perhaps, the costs of providing services to populations in Islamic State territory—such basics as electricity, food, and water, among others—would become prohibitively high for the group. After all, even at its wealthiest, the Islamic State's gross domestic product would only have been approximately the size of some the small economies in Africa, making the Islamic State a rich terrorist group but a poor nation-state.[3] However, the idea that the group eventually would have imploded short of a massive military campaign against it is far from certain. Throughout its existence, the

---

[1] Johnston et al., 2016, pp. 227–233.

[2] See, for example, Jacob N. Shapiro's related research: Jacob N. Shapiro and Janet Hansen-Lewis, "Understanding the Daesh Economy," *Perspectives on Terrorism*, Vol. 9, No. 4, August 2015; Jacob N. Shapiro, "A Predictable Failure: The Political Economy of the Decline of the Islamic State," *CTC Sentinel*, Vol. 9, No. 9, September 2016.

[3] Shapiro and Hansen-Lewis, 2015; Shapiro, 2016; Noack, 2014.

Islamic State and its predecessor groups showed an ability to moderate expenses to match revenues. And there is little indication that the group cared enough about the welfare of inhabitants of its territories to maintain levels of public services at the expense of group strength and cohesion.

Expenditures by Islamic State Predecessor Groups

A large number of documents detailing the expenditures of the Islamic State's predecessor groups are available and have been analyzed.[4] Research on its predecessor groups provides useful context for understanding the opportunities and challenges it faces in bankrolling its ambitious program of jihad and state-building. Analysis of detailed internal financial documents reveals several important spending patterns that have recurred over time and space and thus help establish a general understanding of the group's costs and its efforts to maintain itself in a variety of security conditions.

Throughout the Islamic State's early history as AQI and ISI, the group reallocated money from the components that raised it to those that needed it. The central administration of Anbar Governorate in 2005 and 2006 received revenue from the sector-level administrations, akin to Iraqi districts, and then reallocated it. These reallocations were strongly related to the pace of attacks occurring in the sectors.[5] Later, when ISI was operating from Mosul in 2008 and 2009, it reallocated money throughout Iraq and even to Syria.[6]

Al-Qa'ida in Iraq in Anbar Governorate

Records from the provincial administration in Anbar Governorate, Iraq, from 2005 to 2006, show expenditures of almost $8.5 million and revenues of $9.0 million, for a small surplus. We cannot say that AQI ran an overall surplus because there might have been higher expendi-

---

4 Bahney, Shatz, et al., 2010, pp. 34, 42–43; Johnston et al., 2016, pp. 227–233.

5 Bahney, Shatz, et al., 2010.

6 Johnston et al., 2016.

tures relative to lower revenues before or after that period. Overall, it appears that AQI generally matched spending to revenues.[7]

Of the $8.5 million, 56 percent of provincial expenditures went directly to the sectors. We assess that sectors were responsible for payroll for members in their sector, as well as for a number of other purchases. However, the provincial administration also made a variety of purchases. These included administrative activities, which accounted for 11 percent of spending; military activities, including a military battalion and procurement, which accounted for 10 percent of spending; payroll and medical expenses purely at the provincial level, which accounted for 5 percent of spending; and a number of other tasks, such as media, mail, and activities related to borders, each of which accounted for 2 percent or less of spending. Notably, the provincial administration allocated 9 percent of its spending to the General Treasury. This may have been a provincial reserve fund but could also have been an allocation to overall AQI headquarters. Such an allocation can be found in later data, from 2008 and 2009.

Another notable pattern was that the provincial administration reallocated money within Anbar. For example, Fallujah, the site of pitched battles during this period, accounted for only $104,000 in revenue transferred to the provincial administration but more than $1 million in transfers from the provincial administration.[8] In contrast, the sectors in the relatively peaceful far west of Anbar Governorate had revenue totals much closer to, and sometimes exceeding, expenditures.

Islamic State of Iraq in Ninewa Governorate

Records from the ISI administration in Ninewa Governorate, Iraq, from late 2008 to early 2009, show expenditures of almost $4.5 million and revenues of $4.8 million, for a small surplus. As with finances in Anbar Governorate three years earlier, we cannot say that ISI ran an overall surplus, since there might have been higher expenditures relative

[7] This section is drawn from Bahney, Shatz, et al., 2010, and Johnston et al., 2016, and documents referenced in those two reports.

[8] Bahney, Shatz, et al., 2010.

to lower revenues before or after that period. Overall, it appears that ISI, the successor to AQI, continued to match spending to revenues.[9]

In Anbar Governorate, the AQI sector administrations, rather than the central, provincial administration, were responsible for payroll, but in Ninewa, the ISI central administration was responsible for payroll, so the Mosul central administration's spending profile was somewhat different from that of the Anbar central administration in the earlier period. Of the $4.5 million, 39 percent was spent on salaries and rental support for members without their own houses. Military expenses accounted for 10 percent of total spending, and 5 percent went to the detainee committee, which spent money on legal fees and bribes to obtain favorable outcomes in the Iraqi legal system for detained ISI members. Another 5 percent was spent specifically on weapons. Numerous other categories, such as vehicle purchases, media, and sharia [Islamic law] courts accounted for smaller amounts.

Notably, ISI varied its payments by month depending on revenue. This is best seen in payments for salaries and rents. One would not expect high levels of variation with a monthly payroll. However, for the five full months with available data (September 2008 through January 2009), monthly payroll varied from $478,000 in September to $184,000 in November. September was also the month with the highest level of revenue, and November was the month with the lowest level. While the *level* of salary and rent payments varied a great deal, the amount as a proportion of total revenue stayed between 29 percent and 37 percent for four of the five months.[10]

One other document captured from senior ISI leader Abu Qaswarah in October 2008 also sheds light on ISI spending during this period.[11] This document accounted for ISI finances throughout its

---

[9] This section is drawn from Bahney, Shatz, et al., 2010, and Johnston et al., 2016, and documents referenced in those two reports.

[10] Johnston et al., 2016. Salary figures are derived from the data underlying Figure 8.7, p. 202, and Figure 8.15, p. 218.

[11] Abu Qaswarah, whose real name was Mohamed Moumou and who was also known as Abu Sara, was a top ISI operational leader and possibly the group's number three leader, although, at the time, he was thought to be the second in command. See Ernesto Londoño, "No. 2 Leader of Al-Qaeda in Iraq Killed," *Washington Post*, October 16, 2008; and Bill

entire territory, rather than just in Mosul or Ninewa Governorate. A specific document of revenues and transfers shows that the central ISI administration was actively reallocating money to support group activities throughout its entire territory. During this one snapshot in time, the central treasury received the bulk of its revenue from activities in Baghdad, Mosul, and the desert region southwest of Mosul, known as the Jazirah. Total revenue amounted to $421,000. In turn, it transferred revenue everywhere else, including Anbar, Basra, Diyala, Kirkuk, and Salah al-Din governorates in Iraq, returned some to Baghdad, and sent a small amount to Syria. Total transfers amounted to $667,200.[12]

Estimates of Islamic State Expenditures After 2014

Details about recent Islamic State expenditures are hard to come by, but there have been several credible reports both in the news media and from research organizations.[13] In addition, a number of documents have been found and analyzed.[14] In this section, we discuss highlights of Islamic State spending since 2014.

In late 2015, as the Islamic State was coming under much more effective attack, *Financial Times* reported spending across a variety

---

Roggio, "Al Qaeda in Iraq's Second in Command Was a Swedish Citizen," *Long War Journal*, October 16, 2008.

12 Johnston et al., 2016, pp. 227–233.

13 Sam Jones and Erika Solomon, "ISIS Inc.: Jihadis Fund War Machine but Squeeze 'Citizens,'" *Financial Times*, December 15, 2015; Michael Weiss, "Leaked ISIS Documents Show Internal Chaos," *Daily Beast*, August 30, 2016; Lister, 2014; Robert Windrem, "ISIS Is the World's Richest Terror Group, But Spending Money Fast," CNBC, March 20, 2015.

14 Callimachi, 2018. See also the "Budget for Month of Rabi' al-Awal 1436 AH [December 2014 to January 2015], Squadron 57, General Finance Administration, Wilayat Halab (Aleppo Province)," 2015, available as "Specimen 33K: Monthly Expenses for an Islamic State Squadron in Aleppo Province," from Aymenn Jawad Al-Tamimi, "Archive of Islamic State Administrative Documents (Continued . . . Again)," webpage, September 17, 2016d.

of categories, based on interviews and documents.[15] Among other expenses, the group

- paid its fighters $35 million to $40 million monthly, of which $20 million went to core fighters and $15 million to $20 million to local fighters and auxiliaries. Estimates from coalition intelligence officials on the exact size of the Islamic State's armies varied, but most agreed that, in its prime, the core force was at least 30,000 strong, with an additional 50,000 to 70,000 split between local members and auxiliary and part-time forces
- paid "tens of millions more" for small munitions and explosives, with additional millions of dollars for other military equipment
- spent $10 million to $15 million monthly on security, including the Islamic law police [Hisba], and the intelligence services [Amni or Amniyat][16]
- spent less than $10 million monthly on social services, such hospitals, other health clinics, and schools
- spent $10 million to $15 million per month on public works and other building projects.

Combined, these spending figures amount to about $900 million to $1.1 billion annually, well below what the Islamic State was reported to be gaining in revenue.

Expenditure Details

This section outlines three main types of expenditures: personnel compensation, military, and governance and services. It draws primarily from documents that researcher Aymenn Jawad al-Tamimi has released, as well as secondary sources.[17] The section on personnel costs

---

15 Jones and Solomon, 2015.

16 This is also sometimes referred to as the Emni.

17 Aymenn Jawad Al-Tamimi, "Archive of Islamic State Administrative Documents," webpage, January 27, 2015a; Aymenn Jawad Al-Tamimi, "Archive of Islamic State Administrative Documents (cont.)," webpage, January 11, 2016a; Al-Tamimi, 2016d; and Aymenn Jawad Al-Tamimi, "Archive of Islamic State Administrative Documents (cont.—IV)," webpage, August 28, 2017. These documents are generally considered to be authentic.

highlights what the organization pays most of its members, as recorded on the personnel rosters of Islamic State units. These are the regular member rosters that have stayed largely the same since the AQI days of the group. The military section is limited to military equipment as much as the data and sources allow but includes some salary data for comparison. The governance and services section includes data on personnel costs, but these can be differentiated from the personnel costs in the first section because they do not represent personnel costs for regular units and but rather the additional costs for the personnel needed to administer territory and conduct government and social service functions. Accordingly, the loss of territory also means that there is no longer a need to pay for such things as the salaries of doctors and nurses serving in hospitals.

Personnel Costs for Regular Islamic State Units

Salaries for members have been the largest single expense, but a wide range of these has been reported, from a base salary of $50 per month for a fighter to above $600 per month for specialists.[18] Documentary evidence suggests that salaries are generally low and in line with what the group paid when it was AQI and ISI. This section provides salary data from personnel rosters that usually do not differentiate people by jobs in the organization and often do not differentiate people by place of origin, instead referring to people by a simple alias.

In 2005 and 2006 in Anbar, members were paid a base salary of 60,000 Iraqi dinars per month, about $41 at the time, and then an additional 30,000 Iraqi dinars per month for each wife or dependent.[19] A document captured in February 2009 from the Ninewa administrative emir indicates that ISI paid fighters a base salary of $50 monthly, with an additional $50 per wife and $25 per child.[20]

---

[18] Clarke et al., 2017.

[19] Bahney, Shatz, et al., 2010.

[20] Johnston et al., 2016, p. 285.

More-recent documents indicate that salaries under the Islamic State have stayed about the same.[21] Documents for Islamic State units in Syria show a monthly salary of $50 per fighter, $50 per wife, $50 per parent, and $35 per child.[22] The group also paid $50 per *sabaya* [sex slave], and $35 for each child of a sabaya.[23] In one case, compensation also included $65 for clothing and other expenses.[24] In another case from Aleppo, dating from late December 2014 through most of January 2015, compensation to fighters for wives, children, parents, sabaya, and children of sabaya was the same as above, but fighters were paid $90 per month; it appears this comprised $50 for a salary and $40 for expenses.[25] Documents from Iraq show a similar salary schedule.[26] Specifically, they record 64,000 Iraqi dinars per month for members,

---

[21] Aymenn Jawad Al-Tamimi has posted an archive of Islamic State documents. Among these are "Specimen 14U: Salary Scheme Table for Al Bara' bin Malek Battalion Members," from Al-Tamimi, 2016a; "Specimen 17N: Personnel List: Fallujah Area," from Al-Tamimi, 2016a; "Specimen 17O: Personnel List: Fallujah Area (Cont.)," from Al-Tamimi, 2016a; "Specimen 19N: Personnel List: Homs," from Al-Tamimi, 2016a; "Specimen 33K" (Al-Tamimi, 2016d); and "Specimen 33N: Personnel List from Battalion 57, Aleppo Province," from Al-Tamimi, 2016d.

[22] See "Specimen 14U" (Al-Tamimi, 2016a), "Specimen 19N" (Al-Tamimi, 2016a), and "Specimen 33N" (Al-Tamimi, 2016d). Specimen 14U dates from February and March 2015 and is for an Aleppo battalion that was apparently sent to Hasakah Governorate in Syria. Specimen 19N is undated. Specimen 33N has the Islamic date of Safr 1436, which corresponds to November and December 2014.

[23] The Sinjar area of Iraq is home to a large population of members of the Yazidi religion. The Islamic State considers them to be pagans or polytheists ("The Revival of Slavery Before the Hour," *Dabiq*, No. 4, Dhul-Hijjah 1435 [September–October 2014]; Güneş Murat Tezcür, "Three Years Ago, the Islamic State Massacred Yazidis in Iraq. Why?" *Washington Post*, August 15, 2017). Accordingly, when it conquered Sinjar, the Islamic State killed many of the Yazidi men and forced the Yazidi women into sexual slavery; these slaves were known as *sabaya*. Many have been liberated but suffer from deep trauma (Katrin Kuntz, "Sex Slave Legacy: The Children of the Islamic State," *Spiegel Online*, April 14, 2016).

[24] "Specimen 33N" (Al-Tamimi, 2016d).

[25] "Specimen 33K" (Al-Tamimi, 2016d).

[26] "Specimen 17N" (Al-Tamimi, 2016a) and "Specimen 17O" (Al-Tamimi, 2016a). These documents are undated but include people who were born in the 1990s and have wives and children and so are likely from the 2010s. In addition, column headers are missing from the originals and have been supplied by Al-Tamimi.

wives, and parents and 44,800 Iraqi dinars per month for children and other dependents. This is equivalent to about $53 and $37, respectively, about the same as Islamic State salaries in Syria.[27]

To compare these figures, the average monthly earnings of an employee in Syria in 2010 were 11,344 Syrian pounds, the latest year available.[28] This was equivalent to about $246, well above the earnings of the average Islamic State member four and five years later.[29] In Iraq, average monthly income was 237,000 Iraqi dinars.[30] This is equivalent to about $192, well above what most individual members of the Islamic State were paid.[31]

The Islamic State salary schedule, combined with the fact that salaries constituted the largest portion of Islamic State expenses, meant that the organization's expenditures were largely a function of the number of members it had, conditional on the average number of dependents. However, recall from the Mosul documents of 2008 and 2009 that the organization had a practice of withholding or modifying salaries in times of low revenue. In fact, as the Islamic State came under effective attack in 2015 and 2016, it cut salaries. Citing "exceptional circumstances," the Islamic State Treasury announced that all salaries would be cut in half and that no one would be exempted.[32]

---

27 This calculation is based on the 2014 average monthly exchange rate at market prices, 1,214 Iraqi dinars per dollar (Central Bank of Iraq, 2019).

28 International Labour Organization, "Syrian Arab Republic," webpage, 2015.

29 We converted Syrian pounds in 2010 to dollars at a rate of 46.17 pounds per dollar (University of Pennsylvania, Exchange Rate to U.S. Dollar for Syria [FXRATESYA618NUPN], retrieved from FRED, Federal Reserve Bank of St. Louis, updated September 17, 2012).

30 United Nations Development Program, *Iraq Human Development Report 2014: Iraqi Youth: Challenges and Opportunities*, Iraq: Ministry of Planning and Bayt al Hikma, 2014.

31 We converted dinars to dollars at a rate of about 1,232.7, the average monthly market rate for 2012 (Central Bank of Iraq, 2019).

32 "Specimen 12Q: Lowering of Salaries for Fighters by 50%," in Al-Tamimi, 2016a. This was also confirmed in a speech by a senior U.S. Department of the Treasury official in February 2016 (Glaser, 2016a).

Military Expenditures

The existing evidence shows that military expenditures have been the second major Islamic State expenditure type. Data on military expenditures are scarce, and estimates are often based on flawed assumptions about the group's history and operating concepts. One credible estimate in late 2015 held that the group had been spending more than "tens of millions" for military equipment, which would amount to at least $120 million per year.[33]

The Islamic State purchased a range of supplies that had applications to military activities. For example, records for one battalion in Syria from May and June 2015 indicated $700 for night cameras for cars; $3,000 for a generator for a factory making booby traps (likely improvised explosive devices [IEDs]); $3,000 for military field spades to dig holes during an advance; $1,000 worth of field beds for the reconnaissance squadron; $260 for camouflage nets for antiaircraft guns; and even $400 for 200 mosquito nets "because of pests and the nature of the desert."[34] Payments from the Islamic State treasury to Anbar Governorate in Iraq included $824,000 for salary and rent (in Iraqi dinars); $902,000 for expenses (in Iraqi dinars); $203,000 for fuel provisions (in Iraqi dinars); $222,000 for winter clothes (in Iraqi dinars); and $1 million for weapons (in U.S. dollars).[35] For this particular month, weapon purchases amounted to almost 32 percent of the total, while salary and rents amounted to 26 percent and unidentified expenses almost 29 percent.

Governance Costs

Maintaining control of a territorial expanse as large as the United Kingdom is costly. Under the caliphate, the Islamic State's budget expanded to cover its significantly expanded bureaucratic apparatus, which sprawled across its many provinces in Iraq and Syria and other countries

---

[33] Jones and Solomon, 2015. The authors also estimated that monthly security cost $10 million to $15 million, amounting to a yearly cost of $120 million to $150 million.

[34] Specimen 15O: Expenses Request for a Battalion in Sha'aban 1436 AH, Homes Province," from Al-Tamimi, 2016a.

[35] "Specimen 18N: Financial Data on Payments to Personnel in Anbar for Safr 1436 AH," from Al-Tamimi, 2016a.

in which the group had affiliated branches. These governance functions included, in principle, the costs of imposing and enforcing sharia law under the local authority of a sharia emir and included various security elements, such as the Hisba morality police, which enforced the strict Islamist requirements the Islamic State imposed after taking over a location. An example of these expenses appears in an employment announcement in which the Hisba advertised for a veterinary doctor, an accountant, a guard, a health inspector, a butcher who could perform slaughter in accordance with Islamic law, and cleaners.[36]

The Islamic State also administered payments to needy Muslims in their jurisdiction using money collected from the zakat taxes, as described in Chapter Four. There were also expenses for education and health care. The Islamic State maintained clinics and attempted to retain medical professionals, but both people and medical supplies were scarce almost from the start of the group's expanded territorial rule in 2014. According to one report in December 2015,

> hospitals, healthcare and schooling across Isis territory appear to receive less than $10m a month. Deir Ezzor is one of Isis's largest and most carefully administered provinces. Yet the jihadis run just nine hospitals there, each with no more than 50 doctors and nurses paid a maximum of $300 a month—for a provincewide total of just $135,000 a month.[37]

In another account, medical staff were noted to have fled on a large scale, even knowing that their property would be confiscated.[38]

An overall assessment of Islamic State governance and services found economic decline throughout Islamic State territories.[39] Although some of this was due to Islamic State misrule, much of it

---

[36] "Specimen K: Employment Opportunities with Diwan al-Hisbah, Raqqa Province," from Al-Tamimi, 2015a.

[37] Jones and Solomon, 2015.

[38] Al-Tamimi, 2016b.

[39] Robinson et al., 2017.

was due to the military campaign against it.[40] In fact, in some cities it ruled, such as Raqqa and Mosul, its de facto Syrian and Iraqi capitals, markets, agriculture, and industry remained active, if not quite at the levels they would have attained under more legitimate rule.

Expenses After the Territorial Caliphate

At the Islamic State's peak of power and territorial control, it appeared that total annual expenses were on the order of $1 billion. As of early 2019, its revenue-raising capacity has been diminished. But so have its expenses. One expert reported that, as of March 2019, the Islamic State had a fighting force of 5,000 people who needed to be paid, excluding other facilitators who did not receive salaries. He estimated that the group would, accordingly, need about $8 million per month to maintain the insurgency it is now fighting (as discussed in Chapter Six) and that it could easily secure this amount based on the amount of money still in its possession.[41]

Another way to view this is to consider a thought experiment with personnel. Average compensation per fighter in Anbar and Ninewa governorates in 2006 and 2007 was $96 per month, including rents and other expenses.[42] To maintain conservative estimates, suppose that amount was $150 in 2018. In July 2018, the United Nations estimated that there were 20,000 or 30,000 Islamic State members in Iraq and Syria.[43] If the Islamic State still had that number of fighters as of early 2019, its obligated compensation payments would amount to between $3 million and $4.5 million per month in personnel costs, or $36 mil-

---

[40] Robinson et al., 2017.

[41] Conversation with Iraqi expert Hisham al-Hashemi, March 2019.

[42] Based on data from Benjamin W. Bahney, Radha K. Iyengar, Patrick B. Johnston, Danielle F. Jung, Jacob N. Shapiro, and Howard J. Shatz, "Insurgent Compensation: Evidence from Iraq," *American Economic Review: Papers & Proceedings*, Vol. 103, No. 3, May 2013. Iraqi dinar amounts have been converted to dollars at a rate of 1,370.5 to the dollar, the average of the monthly averages for 2006 and 2007, based on data from the Central Bank of Iraq, 2019.

[43] UNSC, 2018.

lion to $45 million annually. This is far lower than the $35 million to $40 million *per month* it was reportedly paying in 2015.[44] And this is likely an upper-bound estimate for two other reasons. First, as evidence from 2008 and 2009 shows, the group does not necessarily meet its promised obligations but instead varies salary payments to match revenues. Second, with the end of the territorial caliphate and the capture or surrender of thousands of its members, the Islamic State may have to pay many fewer people than 20,000 or 30,000. However, also note that the group has a long-running practice of continuing salary payments to families of imprisoned members.

Just as personnel costs are likely to be lower, military expenses are also likely much lower. As will be further discussed in Chapter Six, the Islamic State has shifted from a largely conventional form of offensive warfare to an irregular form of defensive warfare and terrorism. Accordingly, the group's military expenditures are likely to be far lower than in 2014 through 2017, which included major urban battles for Mosul and Raqqa. As a result of this shift, IEDs have become the group's go-to weapon, especially vehicle-borne IEDs.[45] IEDs are relatively cheap to make. Small arms, such as AK-47 rifles, were another weapon of choice for the Islamic State as it transitioned from a territorial caliphate to an insurgency. These weapons have been used, for example, to ambush opposing forces with guerrilla hit-and-run tactics.

Finally, with the loss of territory, governance expenses have also fallen. As the United Nations noted in February 2019: "Although its territorial losses have removed some sources of revenue, it has correspondingly fewer liabilities and is expected to be able to sustain its operations."[46] No longer does the Islamic State need to provide health care, education, street cleaning, or many of the other services that legitimate governments provide. One residual service it may still provide is dispute resolution under Islamic law, perhaps to those who want it or, more likely, to those who may not want it but are still subject to Islamic

---

[44] Jones and Solomon, 2015.

[45] Charlie Winter, "War by Suicide: A Statistical Analysis of the Islamic State's Martyrdom Industry," The Hague: International Centre for Counter-Terrorism, February 2017.

[46] UNSC, 2019.

State influence. Data from its predecessor groups indicate that providing this service was relatively cheap.

Conclusions on Islamic State Expenditures

There has been a striking decline in Islamic State expenditures, given its loss of territory, its decline in revenue, and its organizational adaptation over time from a statelike caliphate to an insurgency. By reorganizing itself as an insurgency, the group has dramatically reduced expenditures in three ways:

- personnel costs
- military costs
- governance costs.

The Islamic State may have overextended itself with its ambitious state-building project, but because it also faced a concerted military attack on nearly all its fronts, this judgment cannot be made definitively. Once it came under siege, it was impossible for the group to allocate all its resources toward fighting because it had to tie up at least some money and manpower in administration and governance. At the same time, the administration of territory also resulted in revenue, so the Islamic State faced a balancing act between allocating resources to the military effort and allocating resources to running the territorial caliphate.

One thing that the Islamic State has proven adept at over time has been balancing its revenues and expenses. Even when the group has been flush with cash, it has remained disciplined, a trait that has served it well during more-austere times. Expenses were closely tracked, and the group held its members accountable through an extensive paper trail and oversight at all levels of the organization. The Islamic State also ensured that organizational survival remained a top priority, reflected in its spending by type, as revealed in its operating budget. Salaries were the top expense, along with military costs (such as training, equipping, logistics, and munitions). Much smaller shares went to media and service provision.

Even with lower revenue and the loss of territory, the Islamic State is still capable of launching complex attacks, as an event in eastern Deir ez-Zor in late November 2018 revealed. In that case, Islamic State forces killed nearly 100 fighters from the U.S.-backed SDF.[47] In the future, albeit on a severely degraded scale, the Islamic State will be able to extract revenue via extortion, corruption, theft, and looting. In Chapter Six, we discuss this future and policy options for dealing with the Islamic State in its new form.

---

47 Sune Engel Rasmussen and Nazih Osseiran, "Islamic State Kills Dozens of U.S.-Backed Fighters in Syria Battle, Monitor Says," *Wall Street Journal*, November 26, 2018.

CHAPTER SIX

Conclusions and Implications

The Islamic State's caliphate was never just territorial. It was always a caliphate of the mind, a vision of an Islamic state that the modern group's leaders imagined to have existed in history and that, were it to exist in reality as its leaders envisioned, would be a regional menace to its neighboring states and a nightmare primarily for the world's Muslims.

For those combating it and for many people who observed it, the Islamic State was a rich terrorist organization but a poor state. Even as the group has far less money coming in as of 2019, it is crucial to recall that the group's expenses are minimal compared to what they were even in 2017, when it was attempting to maintain the last vestiges of its state. With the loss of the territorial caliphate, there is no pseudo-government responsible for the provision of services—health care and education; municipal salaries; and public works, such as trash removal. With a significantly lower operating budget, continued revenue-generating activities and the cash the Islamic State hoarded will provide it with adequate funds to procure materiel and survive as a clandestine terrorist movement with the ability to wage a prolonged campaign of guerilla warfare throughout Iraq and Syria.[1]

If the Islamic State is planning a comeback, which we assess it is, the group will stick with what works—diversifying its financial portfolio to maintain steady access to financing. What such a reemergence will look like is difficult to project, but its ideology of remaining and

[1] Clarke, 2018.

expanding, its track record of reemerging from previous defeat, and its actions at maintaining a presence all suggest reemergence is a goal. There are already hints of it, with the group reorganizing its forces in Iraq around Kirkuk and Hawija, as well as in Badush, Zummar, and Rabia, northwest of Mosul.[2] The Islamic State is regrouping throughout southern Syria as well, particularly around the town of Suwayda, setting up in Deir ez-Zor Governorate, maintaining a presence in areas held by the Syrian government, and conducting nighttime attacks in areas held by the SDF.[3] Although much of the group's leadership has been killed and although regional and international powers will be much more on guard against an overt territorial presence, the group has been considered defeated before. Its knack for fundraising through criminal activities will prove useful as its members seek to extort, kidnap, kill, steal, smuggle, and traffic to obtain the money they need to survive. Controlling territory would facilitate these activities but is far from a prerequisite.

This chapter discusses next steps in combating the Islamic State. It focuses on finance and how the group can continue to raise money to fuel its insurgency. It then discusses broader issues in the campaign because all lines of effort are intertwined. Halting finance will hurt the group but is not enough by itself to stop the group from conducting operations and attempting a comeback. Militarily defeating the group will, likewise, not stop the fundraising activities that can support its insurgency. Furthermore, many lines of effort, such as reconstruction, sound governance, and political reconciliation, can dampen the Islamic State's ability to raise money.

---

[2] Aziz Ahmad, "Undefeated, ISIS is Back in Iraq," *New York Review of Books*, February 13, 2019.

[3] Sarah Hunaidi, "ISIS Has Not Been Defeated. It's Alive and Well in Southern Syria," *Foreign Policy*, April 3, 2019; Hassan Hassan, "A Hollow Victory Over the Islamic State in Syria? The High Risk of Jihadi Revival in Deir ez-Zor's Euphrates River Valley," *CTC Sentinel*, Vol. 12, No. 2, February 2019, pp. 1–6.

Rebuilding the Islamic State

The Islamic State is an adaptable and resilient organization. Founded in Iraq in the early 2000s by Abu Musab al-Zarqawi, with its roots in Jordan in the 1990s, the Islamic State has since withstood numerous challenges not only to its effectiveness but also to its very survival. It has remained a persistent threat throughout its history and various organizational incarnations—including those without unilateral control over territory—despite numerous declarations of combat victory by its adversaries.[4]

Consistent and redundant organizational structure has undergirded the Islamic State's resilience. The group is well organized, with a defined bureaucracy and lines of reporting that ensure a modicum of continuity despite high turnover rates among its senior leadership, midlevel bureaucrats, and rank and file. When a senior leader is killed or captured, others are ready to take his place; often, they will have been his deputies.

However, the group is neither monolithic nor rigid, and the autonomy given to its constituent parts increases its ability to adapt quickly to changing circumstances. This adaptability has applied to the Islamic State's financial behavior, with the group taking advantage of a variety of revenue-raising opportunities as circumstances on the ground changed.[5] This adaptability has also applied to the group's production of violence.

As of early 2019, there were clear signs that the Islamic State had regrouped. Throughout Kirkuk Governorate in Iraq, Islamic State fighters have constructed fake checkpoints to ambush Iraqi security forces operating in the area. They also set out to destroy oil tankers and

---

4 Thomas E. Ricks and Karen DeYoung, "Al-Qaeda in Iraq Reported Crippled," *Washington Post*, October 15, 2007; Waleed Ibrahim, "Al Qaeda's Two Top Iraq Leaders Killed in Raid," Reuters, April 19, 2010; Brian Fishman, *Redefining the Islamic State: The Fall and Rise of Al-Qaeda in Iraq*, Washington, D.C.: New America Foundation, August 2011.

5 Bahney, Johnston, and Ryan, 2015; Haid Haid, "The Evolving Economic Model of ISIS Post-Caliphate," Atlantic Council website, July 13, 2017.

target Shia civilians making religious pilgrimages.[6] In Kirkuk and elsewhere, including Diyala and Salahaddin governorates, Islamic State sleeper cells helped organize what analyst Hassan Hassan has called *rasd* [roughly equivalent to scoping, or reconnaissance] of these areas to determine how best to operate before reorganizing small formations of fighters.[7] The group retained the ability to conduct complex surprise attacks in both opposition-held and government-held territory—another indication of a revived insurgency. Even after losing much of its territory, the Islamic State continued its fight against regime forces in Hama Governorate in central Syria. It has also launched counterattacks against proregime forces in Homs Governorate in Syria.

Despite the collapse of the territorial caliphate, the Islamic State has displayed resilience and commitment, signaling a resolve that could help the group engineer a comeback even long after the removal of its state. Abu Bakr al-Baghdadi made a rare appearance in an audio recording from September 2017 where he sought to build morale and call for continued jihad, while praising Islamic State fighters and encouraging them to remain steadfast.[8] Military setbacks and deaths of leaders have had some tangible effects on the morale of remaining fighters, such as an increasing number of Islamic State members who voluntarily surrender. In Iraq, some 500 fighters surrendered in Tal Afar, and 1,000 surrendered in Hawija.[9] But many remain active, and, as shown by an Islamic State suicide attack that killed four Americans in Manbij, Syria, in January 2019, the group remains highly lethal.[10]

The Islamic State has also maintained an ability to recruit new fighters, which helped it sustain itself despite mounting battlefield

---

[6] Qassim Abdul-Zahra and Susannah George, "Islamic State Haunts Northern Iraq Months After Its Defeat," Associated Press, March 28, 2018; see also Rikar Hussein, "Islamic State Regrouping in Iraqi, Kurdish Disputed Territories," VOA website, March 26, 2018.

[7] Hassan, 2018a.

[8] "'New Baghdadi Tape' Posted by Islamic State Group," BBC News, September 29, 2017.

[9] Rod Nordland, "ISIS Fighters, Having Pledged to Fight or Die, Surrender en Masse," *New York Times*, October 8, 2017.

[10] Nancy A. Youssef and Raja Abdulrahim, "At Least Four Americans Killed in Syria Attack Claimed by the United States," *Wall Street Journal*, January 16, 2019.

casualties.[11] Recruiting has slowed, and new recruits will likely be far more local—Iraqi and Syrian, rather than foreign—because traveling as a foreign fighter from Europe or elsewhere to what remains of the caliphate seems like a losing proposition on every end. But this was exactly the situation facing the Islamic State in its earlier incarnation as ISI.

The Islamic State is now engaged in a low-level insurgency. Insurgencies win by defeating the government and controlling territory in a permanent fashion. Insurgencies that do not win are protracted conflicts without end. The defeat of the Islamic State's caliphate, its overarching political goal, was an important achievement but does not translate directly to the defeat of the insurgency the group has transitioned back to. Continued access to finances can keep the movement alive until it can try to take advantage of government failure in either Iraq or Syria, or yet another country in the region that develops any serious political instability. In this stage, it will play not to lose as a necessary and temporary condition. Were it to return, the group likely would retain its underlying structure and goals. As it continues operations, the Islamic State's ability to survive, even while conducting fewer attacks and occasionally reverting to a quasi-dormant phase, could create an indelible impression of strength among local populations in areas of contested governance.

Finances and the Future of the Islamic State

The Islamic State has demonstrated an ability to rely on a variety of economic approaches to finance its jihad. Despite financial and operational setbacks, it has experience acting as an organization that can operate without territory but organizes and conducts hit-and-run and ambush attacks while acting as a hybrid criminal-terrorist group to raise money. It demonstrated this as ISI in Ninewa from 2008 to 2011, where occasional spasms of violence intimidated the local population

---

[11] Margaret Coker, Eric Schmitt, and Rukmini Callimachi, "With Loss of Its Caliphate, ISIS May Return to Guerrilla Roots," *New York Times*, October 18, 2017.

and commercial actors and enabled the group to raise money through extortion rackets, contract skimming, and a range of other related criminal activities.[12]

Persistent Financial Management Practices

Revenue has varied by place and time, but the organization has always been able to manage finances to match expenses with revenues at worst and to build a surplus at best. Table 6.1 provides basic revenue and expenditure data, and information on revenue sources, for four places and times: AQI in Anbar Governorate in 2005 and 2006, ISI in Ninewa Governorate in late 2008, the entire ISI at one point in 2008, and the Islamic State in 2015.

Aside from the organization's ability to spend carefully to match revenue, four points stand out. First, the group has been creative about developing a diversified revenue stream throughout its existence. Second, it redistributes money throughout the organization. Especially interesting is ISI's ledger in 2008, showing the transfer of $421,000 to headquarters and the transfer of $667,200 out of headquarters throughout Iraq and even to Syria. Third, when possible, it has taken advantage of resources, especially oil. Again referring to the ISI ledger from 2008, we speculate that $600,000 worth of revenue came from oil: The ledger entry is titled "'Ashraf," and Abu 'Ashraf was a pseudonym for Abu Ibrahim, ISI's oil minister at the time. Fourth, revenue took an exponential leap when the group controlled a large territory with millions of people, illustrating the value to it of establishing a physical state. It is true that the numbers are not directly comparable. The figures for Anbar and Ninewa governorates are for parts of the organization, not the entire organization, but the group was at the peak of its power in these areas during these periods. The data from ISI at a point in 2008 indicate that Mosul was the most lucrative area and was one of only two areas that did not need subsidies from the center (the desert area of the Jazirah to the south and west was the other). Given that, it is difficult to conceive that AQI in 2005 and 2006, and ISI in 2008 and 2009, could have raised anything close to $1 billion in a year.

---

[12] Johnston et al., 2016.

Table 6.1
Islamic State Financial Management Through Time, U.S. $ Millions

Location and Period	Revenue	Expenses	Main Sources of Revenue
Anbar Governorate, Iraq June 2005–May 2006	4.5	4.1	Sale of stolen goods Transfers to provincial administration from sectors Spoils and booty Car sales
Ninewa Governorate, Iraq Late August 2008–January 2009	4.8[a]	4.5[b]	Oil Extortion of contracts Spoils Real estate Miscellaneous
ISI One point in 2008	1.1	0.9	Oil Transfers to headquarters from provinces Cement
Islamic State 2015	1,700	1,000	Oil Taxation Extortion Kidnap for ransom Antiquities Sales from businesses Currency arbitrage

SOURCES: Johnston et al., 2016; Jones and Solomon, 2015; sources listed in Table 3.1.
NOTE: We have opted to provide data for Anbar Governorate only through May 2006, even though we have them through November 2006 because the administrator changed starting in June and because revenues were recorded in different categories. Stopping in May also has the benefit of providing a full year of data, making it comparable in time to the revenue gained by the Islamic State in 2015. The revenue and expenses for ISI are from a financial document seized from a raid on the compound of senior leader Abu Qaswarah in October 2009 and are for the entire organization at one point in time.

[a] 11.5 annualized.

[b] 10.8 annualized.

Iraq, the SDF, the United States, and their partners made significant progress at disrupting—and, in some cases, at denying and destroying—the Islamic State's ability to generate, move, and store money starting in late 2015 and continuing through the completion of this report in 2019. However, our assessment is that even further degradation of Islamic State finances would be unlikely to destroy the group. Regardless of organizational structure or future territorial control, the Islamic State's ability to appropriate resources, tax, and extort local populations and commercial activities is likely to provide sufficient revenue for the organization to sustain itself and perhaps regenerate previously lost capabilities in the near and medium terms, if not longer. The operational environment itself will be a self-regenerating resource for jihadists and criminals.

Degrading the group's finances contributed to difficulties it faced en route to the eventual collapse of its physical caliphate in 2017, but the Islamic State is not a business: The group's objective remains to reestablish its version of an Islamic caliphate under its banner. While financing is necessary to achieve this objective, the group's state-building project relies neither on access to credit from a third party nor on continuous generation of large-scale revenue, such as the group enjoyed in 2014 and 2015. On the contrary, like many nonstate armed groups that have sought control over a state throughout history, the Islamic State's strategy involves the extensive use of irregular warfare based on guerilla tactics levied against asymmetrically larger, stronger, and wealthier opponents—insurgency.[13] This insurgency provides the foundation for its territorial conquest and, eventually, rule.

Extorting the Population Based on Personal Data

Moving forward, the group will likely seek to reinvigorate now-dormant revenue streams by extorting populations living in areas where the Iraqi and Syrian governments, or such alternative entities as the Autonomous Administration of North and East Syria (a largely Kurdish-governed entity), maintain little control and can project little force. Even where these governments and authorities can operate, the Islamic State will likely have leverage over people. During the height of the caliphate, as discussed in Chapter Four, Islamic State members collected personal data from the population, including detailed information on assets and income, as well as the addresses of extended family members. An early 2019 United Nations report acknowledged this issue: "There are reports that the group retains intelligence on

---

[13] Kalyvas, 2006; Jason Lyall and Isaiah Wilson III, "Rage Against the Machines: Explaining Outcomes in Counterinsurgency Wars," *International Organization*, Vol. 63, No. 1, 2009.

local communities that could be used in future efforts to extort or otherwise extract financing from areas previously under its control."[14] With access to this type of information, the group will be able to rely on organized crime–style activities to intimidate and extort civilians, replenishing its cash reserves in the process.

Taking Advantage of Business and Reconstruction

In addition to extortion, another way the Islamic State can continue to make money without physical territory is by engaging in contract skimming. As the overlapping conflicts in Iraq and Syria wind down, the international community and regional players will be called on to help with the reconstruction of devastated cities. The Islamic State's predecessor organizations, AQI and ISI, extorted construction companies and other entities as they worked to rebuild cities, towns, and villages, especially between 2008 and 2011, in the aftermath of the major spike in sectarian conflict. At no point did these groups control anywhere near the amount of territory the Islamic State once controlled.

The same process could very likely repeat itself over the next several years as reconstruction begins in war-torn areas throughout Iraq and Syria. Substantial infusions of aid dollars, especially if not closely monitored, would be too tempting for the Islamic State to ignore. President Donald Trump has publicly called for Saudi Arabia and other wealthy Gulf States to take the lead in financing Syria's reconstruction.[15] Even standard levels of leakage and corruption could keep the group afloat as it works to rebuild its organization into a more formidable threat. In the past, ISI operatives brokered relationships with local officials connected to reconstruction projects before placing its own members in positions of influence within or adjacent to the supply chain. At various steps during the reconstruction process, ISI members had the opportunity to reap illicit gains. In a manner similar to how mafias work in many countries, the jihadists monitor the situation to ensure the work gets completed, although money is earned by taking

---

[14] UNSC, 2019.

[15] Tom O'Connor, "Donald Trump Says Saudi Arabia, Not 'Great Country' U.S., Will Rebuild Syria," *Newsweek*, December 24, 2018.

the difference between the inflated price tag and the remaining funds allocated for the project.

Assets and Other Sources of Revenue

The Islamic State has numerous other sources of revenue. Selling antiquities through smuggling networks and intermediaries remains an option. Kidnap for ransom is practiced and is easier because of the personal data that the group has collected on the population it once ruled. Although donations have never been a large part of its revenue stream, it certainly takes them, and donations will likely continue to flow in, as illustrated by a recent case in Ireland.[16]

Beyond new revenue generation, it is well-established—although, admittedly, not conclusively proven—that the Islamic State has substantial assets, some of which are invested in legitimate businesses and, therefore, expected to provide an ongoing revenue stream for years.[17] The combination of current assets and a future ability to earn money will allow the group to reorganize, regroup, and look for opportunities to return and expand.

Implications for the Counter–Islamic State Campaign

Following its rise to global infamy in 2014, the Islamic State ultimately governed a territory the size of Great Britain. As of March 2019, its territorial caliphate had been destroyed. During its territorial rule, it had amassed a vast war chest, easily making it the wealthiest insurgent group in history. Although there was never any single, agreed-on figure for how much revenue the group was gaining at its peak, it can be said with confidence that the amount was in the billions of dollars during the life of the territorial caliphate. In 2015, for example, as the campaign against it mounted, the group was making at least an estimated $1 million per day from oil alone and a similarly high figure

---

[16] Niall O'Connor, "Gardai Raid 'ISIS Cash Gang' After Tip Off by Bank in Dublin," *Irish Mirror*, January 23, 2019.

[17] "Based in Karbala . . . ," 2018.

from taxation, fees, and extortion.[18] Although the territory is gone, the money is not.

Lines of Effort to Forestall the Return of the Islamic State

Ensuring the demise of the Islamic State will require several intertwined lines of effort: counterterrorism finance, domestic and international intelligence gathering, law enforcement, reconstruction, better government on the part of the conflict states, and military action. In all cases, the United States and international coalition partners can provide essential support.

The most important measures in Iraq and Syria will be domestic intelligence gathering and law enforcement. Authorities will need to identify businesses that have Islamic State investments, the locations of cash storage sites, and money exchange and transfer businesses that are cooperating with the Islamic State. Identifying the businesses with Islamic State investments can lead law enforcement officials to the Islamic State financiers and deny the group revenue. Identifying cash storage locations can lead to airstrikes, in coordination with coalition air forces when Iraqi air forces cannot complete the mission.[19] Ground operations to seize the money, although riskier, would preserve the money for use by legitimate governing authorities in Iraq or Syria. Identifying money exchange businesses can lead to making the transfer of Islamic State funds more difficult; the group's record indicates that it transfers money where needed for its military efforts and that these transfers do result in heightened military activity. This will not completely stop such transfers but could move them to a more vulnerable delivery mechanism, physical couriers.

Measures against Islamic State–linked financial institutions will also require international intelligence gathering and the cooperation of countries in the region. Even though donations have not provided a large share of revenue, the group has raised money around the world,

---

[18] Glaser, 2016a; see also Torbati, 2016.

[19] As of late 2018, Iraqi security forces were, with Syrian government permission, operating in Syria.

such as from people in Qatar and other countries in the Gulf.[20] Even as of late 2018, the Islamic State had a "network of money service businesses, hawalas, and financial facilitators funding terrorism across the Middle East."[21]

Besides tracking Islamic State finances directly, law enforcement and domestic intelligence have a role that may be more important: providing security to the population and making sure reconstruction funds are not extorted. As noted especially in Chapter Four, the Islamic State gathered information on the many people it ruled during the time of the territorial caliphate. Given its past record, it has likely retained much of this information, leaving potentially millions of people vulnerable. Law enforcement and domestic intelligence will need to protect the population from informal taxation (perhaps better considered extortion) and kidnapping. They will also need to ensure an environment in which people feel safe reporting Islamic State activities to authorities for further action. Protecting the population will also require making sure the Islamic State cannot skim or participate in reconstruction contracts. With billions of dollars likely to be spent throughout Iraq and, eventually, Syria, the group will likely dedicate substantial resources and energy to determining how it can extort some portion of that money.[22]

Reconstruction can also help lower the chances of the return of the Islamic State. People have joined the Islamic State and other terrorist groups for a variety of reasons. Although there is a weak link between

---

[20] In September 2014, the U.S. Department of the Treasury sanctioned Tariq Bin-Al-Tahar Bin Al Falih Al-'Awni Al-Harzi, who

> worked to help raise funds from Gulf-based donors for ISIL. In September 2013, he arranged for ISIL to receive approximately $2 million from a Qatar-based ISIL financial facilitator, who required that Al-Harzi use the funds for military operations only. The Qatar-based ISIL financial facilitator also enlisted Al-Harzi's assistance with fundraising efforts in Qatar. (U.S. Department of the Treasury, "Treasury Designates Twelve Foreign Terrorist Fighter Facilitators," press release, Washington, D.C., September 24, 2014)

[21] U.S. Department of the Treasury, "Treasury Targets Iraq-Based Money Service Business Supporting ISIS," press release, Washington, D.C., October 17, 2018b.

[22] Bahney, Johnston, and Ryan, 2015.

poverty and adherence to terrorist groups, financial need does cause some people to join. Accordingly, effective stabilization and reconstruction will be important elements in safeguarding Iraq and Syria from the return of the Islamic State.[23] In cooperation with the international community, the Iraqi government has taken halting steps toward reconstruction. Syria, still at war, is an entirely different case. Even were peace to come, it is unlikely that the United States and the European Union and, following their lead, the World Bank, would provide money for reconstruction if Bashar al-Assad were to remain in power. Money would therefore need to come from Gulf countries, which may provide it; China, which may lend it in the right circumstances; or Russia or Iran, which are unlikely to have money to give or lend.

Related to reconstruction, ensuring the Islamic State does not return will also require better government, especially on the parts of the governments of Iraq and Syria. The return of the group from 2009 through 2013 had multiple causes, but perceptions of an unfair and predatory government in Iraq played a role. In one of the most notorious incidents, in April 2013, the Iraqi army attacked a protest in Sunni Arab Hawijah, killing 50 and injuring 110 and leading to increased demonstrations against the government.[24] At the time, it was reported that

> [m]any Iraqi leaders are now worried that militant groups will capitalize on the anger and disenfranchisement of the Sunni community—and the government's heavy-handed response—to transform a relatively peaceful protest movement into an armed insurrection.[25]

In Iraq, the government of Haider al-Abadi after 2014 and the new government of Adel Abd-al-Mahdi appear to have taken steps toward

---

[23] A valuable guide to stabilization and reconstruction in Iraq is Shelly Culbertson and Linda Robinson, *Making Victory Count After Defeating ISIS: Stabilization Challenges in Mosul and Beyond*, Santa Monica, Calif.: RAND Corporation, RR-2076-RC, 2017.

[24] Even if ISIS elements were involved, the response was viewed as heavy handed. See Patrick Cockburn, "Iraqi Army Losing Hold on North to Sunni and Kurdish Forces as Troops Desert," *Independent*, April 28, 2013.

[25] Kamaran Al-Najar, Patrick Osgood, and Staff, "Kurdish Troops Advance on Kirkuk," *Iraq Oil Report*, April 30, 2013.

treating all communities fairly. However, there are worrying signs that not all is going well, such as the treatment of people suspected of having been involved with the Islamic State and stalled progress in such cities as Mosul.[26] People forced to cooperate with the Islamic State may face a double threat. On the one hand, Islamic State elements may blackmail them by threatening to report them to government authorities. On the other hand, they may face legal jeopardy from government officials or acts of revenge from the Shia-dominated (and, in some cases, Iran-dominated) militias known as the Popular Mobilization Units, or even by less-formal groups or people who have been wronged by the Islamic State.[27] Roundups by the Popular Mobilization Units and arrests, raids, and actions at checkpoints by regular Iraqi government forces in areas formerly dominated by the Islamic State could exacerbate existing tensions and lead to renewed grievances among Sunni Arabs who have returned to these areas.[28] In a survey of 200 women in Anbar Governorate in 2018, more than one-fifth identified the "bad political and economic situation in society" as a cause of extremism in Anbar (tied for first among causes), and 40 percent said the Iraqi government had contributed negatively to reducing extremism in Iraq.[29] Efforts at reconciliation and even some type of amnesty for people who pose no future threat may help actually forestall a future threat stemming from grievances leading to people sympathizing with the Islamic State.

Government trends are far more negative in Syria. There, with Russian airpower, the Assad government's military campaign has included extensive bombings of civilian areas and the use of chemical weapons. The government appears to have engaged in a systematic

---

[26] Ben Taub, "Iraq's Post-ISIS Campaign of Revenge," *New Yorker*, December 24, 2018.

[27] The Popular Mobilization Units, constituted of multiple units, formally formed in 2014 as the Islamic State threatened Baghdad and the Iraqi Army failed to perform adequately. Some existed previously as insurgent groups acting against U.S. troops. Since then, they have been formally incorporated into the structure of the Iraqi Security Forces.

[28] Ahmad, 2019.

[29] Iraqi Organization for Women and Future and Kvinna, *Research Survey Report on More Safety to Al-Anbar Women Project with Decision (1325)*, Baghdad, Iraq, 2018.

campaign of mass murder.[30] In addition, the government has taken steps to expropriate the property of people who have opposed it or are just refugees or internally displaced (the last two groups include at least half the country's prewar population).[31] In some cases, houses and apartments have been offered to Shia foreign fighters from Afghanistan, Pakistan, Iraq, and Lebanon.

In both countries, determining what to do with former and suspected members of the Islamic State will prove a challenge. In Iraq, thousands of people are held in detention centers for suspicion of fighting with or otherwise supporting the Islamic State. In Syria, the SDF hold thousands of Islamic State–linked prisoners. A related challenge will be what to do with the many women and children who were associated with the Islamic State, especially children who have known little else or have a poor memory of life before the Islamic State. Some have proved to be security threats and have carried out attacks.[32]

Finally, military action will still be required. The war against the Islamic State showed the limits of counterterrorism financing. Sanctions, one of the principal traditional tools for this area of policy, were insufficient at halting the advance of the territorial caliphate, and even the strikes on oil infrastructure and cash storage hurt, but did not stop, the group. Military action will still be needed, at minimum, to capture or kill the many Islamic State cells throughout Iraq and Syria, to guard borders, and to hold territory that may be at risk of recapture.

The U.S. and International Role in Forestalling the Return of the Islamic State

The United States must balance two competing issues. The first is that there is little desire for endless military engagement, regardless of the

---

[30] Louisa Loveluck and Zakaria Zakaria, "Syria's Once-Teeming Prison Cells Are Being Emptied by Mass Murder," *Washington Post*, December 23, 2018.

[31] Maha Yahya, "The Politics of Dispossession," Diwan, Carnegie Middle East Center, May 9, 2018.

[32] Joana Cook and Gina Vale, *From Daesh to 'Diaspora': Tracing the Women and Minors of Islamic State*, London: International Centre for the Study of Radicalisation, Department of War Studies, King's College, 2018.

legal foundations for that engagement. The second is that the United States has been essential to the fight against the Islamic State, and continued engagement will likely be necessary to forestall its return. This engagement need not necessarily feature military action prominently, but a military role will likely be needed. In addition, working with international partners is likely to strengthen U.S. efforts.

The essential role for the United States is to continue its activities related to Islamic State finances. This has intelligence, military, and training components. This role will include tracing Islamic State money flows, sanctioning Islamic State financiers and financial institutions linked to the Islamic State, and working with regional central banks and financial intelligence units in this effort. To date, this has been a multinational effort, with both the Counter-ISIS Finance Group, led by Italy, Saudi Arabia, and the United States, and the Paris-based Financial Action Task Force. Because of its central role in the global financial system, its various legal authorities, the skill of its financial intelligence efforts, and its long experience, the United States will need to remain involved.

Countering Islamic State finances may also involve a military component. The group's finances—and the group itself—have been degraded in the past by actions to capture or kill group members and by airstrikes on its facilities and cash storage sites. Actions to capture or kill have sometimes uncovered document troves that provided valuable evidence of financing activities and that have led to further actions against the group. Similar intelligence could prove invaluable to efforts to prevent the group from returning.

The United States and its international partners also have a role in law enforcement training and funding. Italy has played a leading role in this effort in Iraq, training more than 13,000 police officers through spring 2018 and working with Iraq on antiquities protection.[33] The United States need not take the lead but should be available in support of international partners.

---

33 Elisabeth Braw, "For Not-Quite-Wars, Italy Has a Useful Alternative to Traditional Troops," Defense One website, April 16, 2018b.

International involvement is likely to be essential to stabilization and reconstruction in Iraq and Syria. Such involvement would include, at minimum, financing and assistance with ensuring that reconstruction funds do not leak to the Islamic State. Oversight to provide donors with the assurance that the money is not being wasted will also be helpful. Although it need not take the lead, U.S. involvement in these aspects will be helpful to the recipient countries and will benefit the United States by lowering the probability of an Islamic State comeback. Oversight of funding and financial assistance continuously prove to be a challenge, especially in war zones, and the United States learned critical lessons through following the money and attempting to rein in corruption and waste over the past two decades in Afghanistan and Iraq.

Several aspects of military involvement will remain important. The United States has been a valuable partner in the training and operations of the Iraqi Security Forces. They will need continued assistance, and U.S. involvement will not only help them but could forestall degradation and politicization and work to guard against increasing sectarianism, as happened in the years before the Islamic State conquered Mosul. Certainly, if the Iraqi government calls on the United States to end its involvement, the United States should go. But the Iraqi government is also fully aware of the state of its armed forces before the return of the Islamic State and of the capabilities and contribution of the United States.

The different situations in Iraq and Syria also underline why U.S. military involvement may continue to be necessary. Although Iraq faces serious problems, a recognized, legitimate government presides over the country and is able both to formulate national policy and to work with international partners. Continuing to train Iraqi forces and partnering with them is likely to prove effective at continuing to degrade the Islamic State in Iraq.

Syria is entirely different. Even though the UNSC has unanimously endorsed "a Syrian-led, Syrian-owned political transition to end the conflict," there is no sign of any political transition.[34] As of

[34] United Nations, "Security Council Unanimously Adopts Resolution 2254 (2015), Endorsing Road Map for Peace Process in Syria, Setting Timetables for Talks," SC/12171, December 18, 2015b.

January 2019, the country was split between a regime-ruled zone in the west; a semiautonomous zone in the northeast governed by Syrian Kurds; a section in the northwest governed by Turkey; and another section in the northwest with oversight by Turkey but dominated by Hayat Tahrir al-Sham, formerly Jabhat al-Nusra, a terrorist group that, at one time, had overt links to al-Qa'ida.[35]

The bulk of the serious fighting against the Islamic State has been carried out by the SDF, a Kurdish Arab force built around the Kurdish YPG. Complicating future planning efforts, the YPG has strong links to the Kurdistan Workers Party [Partiya Karkeren Kurdistan], which has been battling Turkey for decades. The United States and Turkey, a North Atlantic Treaty Organization ally, have designated the Kurdistan Workers Party as a terrorist group. The U.S. partnership with the SDF came about largely because the Turkish government had not been helpful against the Islamic State and because the YPG proved an effective fighting force. This issue continues to be a sticking point between the Trump administration and Turkey's president, Recep Tayyip Erdoğan, who views support to the Kurds as state-sponsored support for terrorism.

Given the current location of the Islamic State and the way it has maintained its organization and resurged in the past, U.S. involvement with the SDF will likely be necessary until a legitimate government takes over Syria, a process that could take years to unfold and stabilize. The Islamic State and its predecessors have long relied on the desert area straddling Iraq and Syria, the Jazirah, to serve as a hideout and a location from which to rebuild.[36] While Iraqi security forces can act against the Islamic State in the Iraqi portions of the Jazirah and even conduct cross-border operations, Turkish forces will likely find it difficult to operate in the Syrian portions, far south of their border with Syria. Syrian regime forces may spark opposition from the Sunni Arab

---

[35] Jabhat al-Nusra is the group that ISI covertly seeded in Syria toward the start of that country's civil war. See also, Nisan Ahmado, "Experts Fear Terror Group Consolidating Power in Syria," Voice of America, January 25, 2019.

[36] Weiss and Hassan, 2016.

populations of the area, and Iranian forces and their proxies would be likely to spark even more opposition.

It may be that the Syrian Kurds, who have not been opponents of the Assad regime, could strike a deal, gain some form of autonomy, and thus be able to carry on the counter–Islamic State campaign with support from the Syrian national government. However, the Turkish government would likely be strongly opposed to a semiautonomous, armed Kurdish entity on the southern border of Turkey. All this suggests that U.S. forces would be useful as a stabilizing force until the regional players reached some form of accommodation. Although not certain, a complete U.S. pullout would likely result in competition among the Syrian Kurds, Turkey, and the Syrian central government and its allies that would give an opening for the Islamic State to strengthen and return. One option would be to strengthen checkpoints and joint patrols between the U.S. and Kurdish forces operating in the area. This could bring a modicum of stability, although such patrols could result in attacks on American troops. Such a role could also be played by a multinational force replacing U.S. forces, but creating such a force has proven difficult, at least as of April 2019.

In a fluid security environment with limited ability or willingness to conduct the type of policing activities that would deter widespread criminality, Islamic State members will once again try to resuscitate a shadow economy in the rural Sunni heartlands. The group has a proven track record of doing so successfully. And unlike before 2014, it likely has hundreds of millions of dollars and extensive data on the population, its tribal structure and alliances, and its assets. A resuscitated Islamic State will represent a danger to the region, U.S. allies, and even the United States. Given the unsettled security situation, the Islamic State's capabilities, and the value of military action to degrade Islamic State finances, this points to the potential need for continued U.S. military participation.

Abbreviations

AQI	Tanzhim al-Qa'ida fi Bilad al-Rafidain [The Organization of the Base of Jihad in Mesopotamia], also known as al-Qa'ida in Iraq
CJTF-OIR	Combined Joint Task Force–Operation Inherent Resolve
Daesh	Pejorative acronym for the Arabic name for ISIS: al-Dawlah al-Islamiyah fil al-Iraq wa al-Sham
IED	improvised explosive device
ISI	Islamic State of Iraq
ISIL	Islamic State in Iraq and the Levant, same as ISIS
ISIS	Islamic State in Iraq and Syria [or al-Sham], same as ISIL
PAO	Public Affairs Office
SDF	Syrian Democratic Forces
UK	United Kingdom
UNSC	United Nations Security Council
YPG	People's Protective Units [Yekîneyên Parastina Gel]

References

Abdulrahim, Raja, "In Syria's Mangled Economy, Truckers Stitch Together Warring Regions," *Wall Street Journal*, May 24, 2016.

Abdul-Zahra, Qassim, and Susannah George, "Islamic State Haunts Northern Iraq Months After Its Defeat," Associated Press, March 28, 2018.

Abu Hanieh, Hassan, and Mohammad Abu Rumman, *The Islamic State Organization: The Sunni Crisis and the Struggle of Global Jihadism*, trans. Banan Malkawi, Amman, Jordan: Friedrich Ebert Stiftung, 2015.

al-Adnani ash-Shami, Abu Muhammad, "That They Live By Proof," AlHayat Media Center, 2016 (accessed from a website run by scholar Pieter Van Ostaeyen).

Ahmad, Aziz, "Undefeated, ISIS is Back in Iraq," *New York Review of Books*, February 13, 2019. As of April 6, 2019:
https://www.nybooks.com/daily/2019/02/13/undefeated-isis-is-back-in-iraq/

Ahmado, Nisan, "Experts Fear Terror Group Consolidating Power in Syria," Voice of America, January 25, 2019.

Almukhtar, Sarah, "ISIS Finances Are Strong," *New York Times*, May 19, 2015. As of April 24, 2018:
https://www.nytimes.com/interactive/2015/05/19/world/middleeast/isis-finances.html

AlMukhtar, Sarah, Troy Griggs, K. K. Rebecca Lai, and Tim Wallace, "The Islamic State: From Insurgency to Rogue State and Back," *New York Times*, October 22, 2017. As of December 10, 2018:
https://www.nytimes.com/interactive/2017/10/22/world/middleeast/isis-the-islamic-state-from-insurgency-to-rogue-state-and-back.html

Al-Qa'ida in Iraq, "Income and Outcome Report for Al-Anbar Province in Iraq 2," NMEC-2007-633700, 2006 (hosted on the Combating Terrorism Center at West Point website). As of January 15, 2019:
https://ctc.usma.edu/harmony-program/income-and-outcome-report-for-al-anbar-province-in-iraq-2-original-language/

Al-Qa'ida in Iraq, "Income and Outcome Report for Al-Anbar Province in Iraq 4," NMEC-2007-633919, 2006 (hosted on the Combating Terrorism Center at West Point website). As of January 16, 2019:
https://ctc.usma.edu/harmony-program/income-and-outcome-report-for-al-anbar-province-in-iraq-4-original-language/

"Analysis of the State of ISI" (English trans.), Combating Terrorism Center at West Point Harmony Program website, NMEC-2007-612449, undated. As of May 3, 2017:
https://www.ctc.usma.edu/posts/analysis-of-the-state-of-isi-english-translation-2

AQI—*See* Al-Qa'ida in Iraq.

Arango, Tim, "Top Qaeda Leaders in Iraq Reported Killed in Raid," *New York Times*, April 19, 2010. As of February 8, 2017:
http://www.nytimes.com/2010/04/20/world/middleeast/20baghdad.html

Bahney, Benjamin W., Radha K. Iyengar, Patrick B. Johnston, Danielle F. Jung, Jacob N. Shapiro, and Howard J. Shatz, "Insurgent Compensation: Evidence from Iraq," *American Economic Review: Papers & Proceedings*, Vol. 103, No. 3, May 2013, pp. 518–522. As of May 15, 2019:
https://www.jstor.org/stable/23469786?seq=1#metadata_info_tab_contents

Bahney, Benjamin, Patrick B. Johnston, and Patrick Ryan, "The Enemy You Know and the Ally You Don't," *Foreign Policy*, June 23, 2015. As of April 24, 2018:
http://foreignpolicy.com/2015/06/23/the-enemy-you-know-and-the-ally-you-dont-arm-sunni-militias-iraq/

Bahney, Benjamin, Renny McPherson, and Howard J. Shatz, "Glimpse of Bin Laden Techniques in Captured Records of al-Qa'ida in Iraq," Sitrep, GlobalSecurity.org website, May 27, 2011.

Bahney, Benjamin, Howard J. Shatz, Carroll Ganier, Renny McPherson, Barbara Sude, Sara Beth Elson, and Ghassan Schbley, *An Economic Analysis of the Financial Records of al-Qa'ida in Iraq*, Santa Monica, Calif.: RAND Corporation, MG-1026-OSD, 2010. As of March 30, 2017:
https://www.rand.org/pubs/monographs/MG1026.html

Bakker, Edwin, and Mark Singleton, "Foreign Fighters in the Syria and Iraq Conflict: Statistics and Characteristics of a Rapidly Growing Phenomenon," in Andrea de Guttry, Francesca Capone, and Christophe Paulussen, eds., *Foreign Fighters Under International Law and Beyond*, The Hague: T.M.C. Asser Press, 2016, pp. 9–25.

Barclay, Jack, "Al-Tatarrus: al-Qaeda's Justification for Killing Muslim Civilians," *Jamestown Terrorism Monitor*, Vol. 8, No. 34, September 9, 2010. As of January 2, 2019:
https://jamestown.org/program/al-tatarrus-al-qaedas-justification-for-killing-muslim-civilians/

Barnard, Anne, and Hwaida Saad, "Raqqa, ISIS 'Capital,' Is Captured, U.S.-Backed Forces Say," *New York Times*, October 17, 2017. As of January 26, 2019: https://www.nytimes.com/2017/10/17/world/middleeast/isis-syria-raqqa.html

"Based in Karbala . . . Nas Discloses Details of the 'Al-Rawi Network' Implicated in Funding 'Daesh,'" Nas News (in Arabic), November 5, 2018. As of January 20, 2019:
https://www.nasnews.com/مقرها-كربلاء-ناس-يكشف-تفاصيل-شبكة-ال/

Bindner, Laurence, and Gabriel Poirot, *ISIS Financing in 2015*, Paris: Center for the Analysis of Terrorism, May 2016. As of December 10, 2018:
http://cat-int.org/index.php/2016/06/01/
isis-financing-in-2015-report-and-summary/?lang=en

Bird, Mike, "The Syrian Pound's Black Market Moves Are a Futures Contract on Bashar Al Assad," *Wall Street Journal*, April 1, 2016. As of April 8, 2019:
https://blogs.wsj.com/moneybeat/2016/04/01/
the-syrian-pounds-black-market-moves-are-a-futures-contract-on-bashar-al-assad/

Black, Ian, Rania Abouzeid, Mark Tran, Shiraz Maher, Roger Tooth, and Martin Chulov, "The Terrifying Rise of Isis: $2bn in Loot, Online Killings and an Army on the Run," *Guardian*, June 16, 2014.

Braw, Elisabeth, "For Not-Quite-Wars, Italy Has a Useful Alternative to Traditional Troops," Defense One website, April 16, 2018. As of January 28, 2019:
https://www.defenseone.com/ideas/2018/04/
todays-not-quite-wars-italy-has-alternative-traditional-troops/147457/

Brisard, Jean-Charles, and Damien Martinez, *Islamic State: The Economy-Based Terrorist Funding*, ThomsonReuters Accelus, October 2014.

Bunzel, Cole, "From Paper State to Caliphate: The Ideology of the Islamic State," Washington, D.C.: Brookings Institution, The Brookings Project on U.S. Relations with the Islamic World Analysis Paper No. 19, March 2015. As of February 27, 2017:
https://www.brookings.edu/wp-content/uploads/2016/06/The-ideology-of-the-Islamic-State.pdf

———, "A House Divided: Origins and Persistence of the Islamic State's Ideological Divide," *Jihadica*, June 5, 2018a.

———, "The Islamic State's Mufti on Trial: The Saga of 'Silsila 'Ilmiyya,'" *CTC Sentinel*, Vol. 11, No. 9, October 2018b.

Burns, John F., and Kirk Semple, "U.S. Finds Insurgency Has Funds to Sustain Itself," *New York Times*, November 26, 2006.

Byman, Daniel, "Divisions Within the Global Jihad: A Primer," *Lawfare*, September 29, 2017. As of January 2, 2019:
https://www.lawfareblog.com/divisions-within-global-jihad-primer

Callimachi, Rukmini, "ISIS Enshrines a Theology of Rape," *New York Times*, August 13, 2015. As of June 24, 2019:
https://www.nytimes.com/2015/08/14/world/middleeast/isis-enshrines-a-theology-of-rape.html

———, "In an email, US-backed Coalition fighting ISIS told me that of the 104,000 square kms the group held in Iraq/Syria, 93790 is liberated," tweet, October 17, 2017. As of December 10, 2018:
https://twitter.com/rcallimachi/status/920451475624677377

———, "The ISIS Files," *New York Times*, April 4, 2018. As of December 11, 2018:
https://www.nytimes.com/interactive/2018/04/04/world/middleeast/isis-documents-mosul-iraq.html

Central Bank of Iraq, "Price Indicators, Exchange Rate, Market Price" online data, 2019. As of January 25, 2019:
http://cbiraq.org/DataValues.aspx?dtFrm=01/01/2004&dtTo=01/25/2019&tmId=390&dtformat=MMM,yyyy

Chulov, Martin, "How an Arrest in Iraq Revealed ISIS's $2bn Jihadist Network," *Guardian*, June 15, 2014. As of April 15, 2018:
https://www.theguardian.com/world/2014/jun/15/iraq-isis-arrest-jihadists-wealth-power

CJTF-OIR PAO—*See* Combined Joint Task Force–Operation Inherent Resolve Public Affairs Office.

Clarke, Colin P., "ISIS's New Plan to Get Rich and Wreak Havoc," *Foreign Policy*, October 10, 2018. As of December 11, 2018:
https://foreignpolicy.com/2018/10/10/isiss-new-plans-to-get-rich-and-wreak-havoc/

Clarke, Colin P., and Haroro J. Ingram, "After the Caliphate Project: Defeating the ISIS Nostalgia Narrative," Foreign Policy Research Institute website, April 18, 2018. As of May 10, 2019:
https://www.fpri.org/article/2018/04/defeating-the-isis-nostalgia-narrative/

Clarke, Colin P., Kimberly Jackson, Patrick B. Johnston, Eric Robinson, and Howard J. Shatz, *Financial Futures of the Islamic State of Iraq and the Levant: Findings from a RAND Corporation Workshop*, Santa Monica, Calif.: RAND Corporation, CF-361, 2017. As of June 1, 2018:
https://www.rand.org/pubs/conf_proceedings/CF361.html

Cockburn, Patrick, "Iraqi Army Losing Hold on North to Sunni and Kurdish Forces as Troops Desert," *Independent*, April 28, 2013.

Cohen, David S., "Attacking ISIL's Financial Foundation," remarks of Under Secretary for Terrorism and Financial Intelligence David S. Cohen at The Carnegie Endowment for International Peace, October 23, 2014a. As of April 11, 2018:
https://www.treasury.gov/press-center/press-releases/Pages/jl2672.aspx

———, "The Islamic State and Terrorist Financing," written testimony for House Financial Services Committee, November 13, 2014b. As of March 30, 2017: https://www.treasury.gov/press-center/press-releases/Pages/jl9697.aspx

Coker, Margaret, "How Islamic State's Secret Banking Network Prospers," *Wall Street Journal*, February 24, 2016. As of January 26, 2019: https://www.wsj.com/articles/how-islamic-states-secret-banking-network-prospers-1456332138

Coker, Margaret, Eric Schmitt, and Rukmini Callimachi, "With Loss of Its Caliphate, ISIS May Return to Guerrilla Roots," *New York Times*, October 18, 2017. As of December 11, 2018: https://www.nytimes.com/2017/10/18/world/middleeast/islamic-state-territory-attacks.html

Coles, Isabel, "Despair, Hardship as Iraq Cuts Off Wages in Islamic State Cities," Reuters, October 2, 2015. As of January 26, 2019: https://www.reuters.com/article/us-mideast-crisis-iraq-salaries/despair-hardship-as-iraq-cuts-off-wages-in-islamic-state-cities-idUSKCN0RW0V620151002

Combined Joint Task Force–Operation Inherent Resolve Public Affairs Office, "Coalition Forces Kill ISIS Financial Facilitator," press release, June 23, 2017. As of December 12, 2018: https://dod.defense.gov/News/Article/Article/1227137/coalition-forces-kill-isis-financial-facilitator/

———, "Coalition Kills Daesh Criminal Leader, Followers," press release, June 19, 2018a. As of December 11, 2018: https://www.centcom.mil/MEDIA/NEWS-ARTICLES/News-Article-View/Article/1554160/coalition-kills-daesh-criminal-leader-followers/

———, "Senior ISIS Facilitators Arrested in Iraq," press release, October 11, 2018b.

———, "CJTF-OIR Continues Partner Support to Defeat ISIS," press release, December 25, 2018c. As of June 7, 2019: https://www.inherentresolve.mil/Media-Library/News-Releases/Article/1720863/cjtf-oir-continues-partner-support-to-defeat-isis/

———, "CJTF-OIR, Partner Forces Further Reduce ISIS Influence," press release, January 15, 2019a. As of June 7, 2019: https://www.inherentresolve.mil/Media-Library/News-Releases/Article/1732232/cjtf-oir-partner-forces-further-reduce-isis-influence/

———, "CJTF-OIR, Partner Forces Liberate Additional Syrian Villages," press release, January 19, 2019b. As of June 7, 2019: https://www.inherentresolve.mil/Media-Library/News-Releases/Article/1736569/cjtf-oir-partner-forces-liberate-additional-syrian-villages/

Cook, Joana, and Gina Vale, *From Daesh to 'Diaspora': Tracing the Women and Minors of Islamic State*, London: International Centre for the Study of Radicalisation, Department of War Studies, King's College, 2018.

Coolsaet, Rik, "Anticipating the Post-Daesh Landscape," Brussels: Egmont—The Royal Institute for International Relations, Egmont Paper 97, October 2017.

Counter Extremism Project, *Nusra Front [Jabhat Fateh al-Sham]*, 2018.

Counter ISIL Finance Group, "Fact Sheet: Taking Stock of the Counter ISIL Finance Group's Achievements in its First Year," April 8, 2016. As of January 19, 2019:
http://www.dt.tesoro.it/export/sites/sitodt/modules/documenti_it/prevenzione_reati_finanziari/antiusura/2016_04_08_CIFG_Fact_Sheet_9_April_2016.pdf

Cronin, Audrey Kurth, "Behind the Curve: Globalization and International Terrorism," *International Security*, Vol. 27, No. 3, Winter 2002/03, pp. 30–58.

Culbertson, Shelly, and Linda Robinson, *Making Victory Count After Defeating ISIS: Stabilization Challenges in Mosul and Beyond*, Santa Monica, Calif.: RAND Corporation, RR-2076-RC, 2017. As of May 13, 2019:
https://www.rand.org/pubs/research_reports/RR2076.html

"Daesh Makes Movements East of Deir Ezzor . . . And Controls Oil Wells in the Area," DeirezZor 24 website, December 28, 2018. As of January 19, 2019:
https://en.deirezzor24.net/daesh-makes-movements-east-of-deir-ezzor-and-controls-oil-wells-in-the-area/

"Daesh's Financing . . . Surprises of the Huge Criminal Network," 218 TV website (in Arabic), December 22, 2018. As of April 2, 2019:
https://www.218tv.net/تمويل-داعش-مفاجآت-شبكة-الإجرام-الضخم/

Dearden, Lizzie, "ISIS Claims to Mint Gold and Silver Coins for Currency Free from 'Satanic' Global Economy," *Independent*, June 24, 2015. As of March 17, 2018:
http://www.independent.co.uk/news/world/middle-east/isis-claims-to-mint-gold-and-silver-coins-for-currency-free-from-satanic-global-economy-10342632.html

"Director of Abi Saida District: Most of the Villages in the South of the District Are Under the Control of Daesh," Al-Sumaria News (in Arabic), January 23, 2019. As of January 26, 2019:
https://www.alsumaria.tv/news/258765/مدير-ناحية-ابي-صيدا-معظم-قرى-جنوب-الناحية-تحت-سيطر

Dodwell, Brian, Daniel Milton, and Muhammad Al-'Ubaydi, "Burying the Lede: The Islamic State Downsizes?" Combating Terrorism Center at West Point website, July 20, 2018. As of April 6, 2019:
https://ctc.usma.edu/burying-lede-islamic-state-downsizes/

"Does ISIS Need Territory to Survive?" *New York Times*, October 21, 2016. As of June 7, 2019:
https://www.nytimes.com/roomfordebate/2016/10/21/does-isis-need-territory-to-survive

Duhaime, Christine, *Terrorist Financing and the Islamic State*, white paper, Duhaime Law website, 2015. As of December 10, 2018:
http://www.duhaimelaw.com/wp-content/uploads/2015/04/White-Paper-Terrorist-Financing-Methods1.pdf

"Dunam," Oxford Living Dictionaries website, 2019. As of April 3, 2019:
https://en.oxforddictionaries.com/definition/dunam

Esposito, John L., ed., *The Oxford Dictionary of Islam*, Oxford: Oxford University Press, 2003 (online edition).

Fanusie, Yaya J., and Alex Entz, "Islamic State Financial Assessment," Washington, D.C.: Foundation for Defense of Democracies, Center on Sanctions and Illicit Finance, March 2017. As of April 16, 2018:
http://www.defenddemocracy.org/content/uploads/documents/Islamic_State_Terror_Finance.pdf

Farooq, Umar, "Raqqa: 'It Is a Very Sad Life Under ISIL,'" Al Jazeera, January 28, 2015.

Fick, Maggie, and Maha El Dahan, "Exclusive: Islamic State Militants Grab New Weapon—Iraqi Wheat," Reuters, August 13, 2014. As of April 6, 2019:
https://www.reuters.com/article/us-iraq-security-islamicstate-wheat/exclusive-islamic-state-militants-grab-new-weapon-iraqi-wheat-idUSKBN0GD14720140813

Field Manual 3-24/Marine Corps Warfighting Publication 3-33.5, *Insurgencies and Countering Insurgencies*, Change 1, Washington, D.C.: Headquarters, Department of the Army, June 2014. As of June 3, 2019:
https://armypubs.army.mil/ProductMaps/PubForm/Details.aspx?PUB_ID=83748

Financial Action Task Force, *Financing of the Terrorist Organization Islamic State in Iraq and the Levant*, Paris, 2015. As of December 10, 2018:
http://www.fatf-gafi.org/publications/methodsandtrends/documents/financing-of-terrorist-organisation-isil.html

Finn, Tom, "Qatar's Channel to Militants Possibly Dangerous, Possibly Useful," Reuters, December 18, 2015. As of May 3, 2017:
http://www.reuters.com/article/us-mideast-crisis-syria-qatar-idUSKBN0U11O220151218

Fishman, Brian, *Dysfunction and Decline: Lessons Learned from Inside Al Qa'ida in Iraq*, West Point, N.Y.: Combating Terrorism Center at West Point, March 16, 2009.

———, *Redefining the Islamic State: The Fall and Rise of Al-Qaeda in Iraq*, Washington, D.C.: New America Foundation, August 2011. As of June 7, 2019: https://static.newamerica.org/attachments/4343-redefining-the-islamic-state/Fishman_Al_Qaeda_In_Iraq.023ac20877a64488b2b791cd7e313955.pdf

———, *The Master Plan: ISIS, Al-Qaeda, and the Jihadi Strategy for Final Victory*, New Haven, Conn.: Yale University Press, 2016.

Fowler, Jennifer, "Remarks of Deputy Assistant Secretary for Terrorist Financing Jennifer Fowler at the Washington Institute for Near East Policy on U.S. Efforts to Counter the Financing of ISIL," Washington, D.C.: U.S. Department of the Treasury, February 2, 2015. As of January 26, 2019: https://www.treasury.gov/press-center/press-releases/Pages/jl9755.aspx

Francis, Ellen, "U.S. Backed Militias Seize Key Oil Field in East Syria: SDF," Reuters, October 22, 2017. As of January 26, 2019: https://www.reuters.com/article/us-mideast-crisis-syria-oilfield/u-s-backed-militias-seize-key-oil-field-in-east-syria-sdf-idUSKBN1CR07E

Furqan Establishment for Media Production, "Informing the People About the Birth of the Islamic State of Iraq: A Research on the Establishment of the Islamic State of Iraq, the Motives for Its Establishment, Its Connection to the Future of the Jihadist March, and Its Important Political Roles," 2006.

Glaser, Daniel, "Remarks by Assistant Secretary for Terrorist Financing Daniel Glaser at Chatham House," Washington, D.C.: U.S. Department of the Treasury, February 8, 2016a. As of December 12, 2018: https://www.treasury.gov/press-center/press-releases/Pages/jl0341.aspx

———, "Testimony of A\S for Terrorist Financing Daniel L. Glaser Before the House Committee on Foreign Affairs Subcommittee on Terrorism, Nonproliferation, and Trade and the House Committee on Armed Services, Subcommittee on Emerging Threats and Capabilities," Washington, D.C.: U.S. Department of the Treasury, June 9, 2016b. As of December 12, 2018: https://www.treasury.gov/press-center/press-releases/Pages/jl0486.aspx

Glazer, Emily, Nour Malas, and Jon Hilsenrath, "U.S. Cut Cash to Iraq on Iran, ISIS Fears, *Wall Street Journal*, November 3, 2015. As of January 26, 2019: https://www.wsj.com/articles/u-s-cut-cash-to-iraq-on-iran-isis-fears-1446526799

Green, R., "Dispute Over Takfir Rocks Islamic State," Middle East Media Research Institute website, August 4, 2017. As of May 13, 2019: https://www.memri.org/reports/dispute-over-takfir-rocks-islamic-state

Greenberg, Jon, "Donald Trump: ISIS Territory Losses Near 100 Percent, Politifact website, January 30, 2018, As of December 10, 2018: http://www.politifact.com/truth-o-meter/statements/2018/jan/30/donald-trump/trump-isis-territory-losses-near-100/

Haid, Haid, "The Evolving Economic Model of ISIS Post-Caliphate," Atlantic Council website, July 13, 2017. As of June 28, 2018:
http://www.atlanticcouncil.org/blogs/syriasource/the-evolving-economic-model-of-isis-post-caliphate

Hamid, Shadi, and Rashid Dar, "Islamism, Salafism, and Jihadism: A Primer," Markaz blog, Washington, D.C.: Brookings Institution, July 15, 2016. As of January 30, 2017:
https://www.brookings.edu/blog/markaz/2016/07/15/islamism-salafism-and-jihadism-a-primer/

Hamming, Tore, "The Extremist Wing of the Islamic State," Jihadica website, June 9, 2016. As of May 13, 2019:
http://www.jihadica.com/the-extremist-wing-of-the-islamic-state/

Hasan, Zubair, "Theory of Profit: The Islamic Viewpoint," *Journal of Research in Islamic Economics*, Vol. 1, No. 1, 1983, pp. 3–14.

Hasanuz Zaman, S. M., "Definition of Islamic Economics," *Journal of Research in Islamic Economics*, Vol. 1, No. 2, 1984, pp. 49–50. As of November 15, 2018:
https://iei.kau.edu.sa/Files/121/Files/153905_Vol-1-2-16E-SMZaman.pdf

Hassan, Hassan, "The Sectarianism of the Islamic State: Ideological Roots and Political Context," paper, Washington, D.C.: Carnegie Endowment for International Peace, June 13, 2016a. As of May 13, 2019:
https://carnegieendowment.org/2016/06/13/sectarianism-of-islamic-state-ideological-roots-and-political-context-pub-63746

———, "The Islamic State After Mosul," *New York Times*, October 24, 2016b. As of April 24, 2018:
https://www.nytimes.com/2016/10/24/opinion/the-islamic-state-after-mosul.html

———, "ISIL Sleeper Cells in Iraq Are a Warning Sign the Extremist Group Is Already Reforming," *National*, March 28, 2018a. As of April 25, 2018:
https://www.thenational.ae/opinion/comment/isil-sleeper-cells-in-iraq-are-a-warning-sign-the-extremist-group-is-already-reforming-1.716800

———, "ISIS Is Ready for a Resurgence," *Atlantic*, August 26, 2018b.

———, *Out of the Desert: ISIS's Strategy for a Long War*, Washington, D.C.: Middle East Institute, Policy Paper 2018-8 September 2018c. As of January 14, 2019:
https://www.mei.edu/sites/default/files/2018-11/PP10_Hassan_ISISCT.pdf

———, "ISIS Is Poised to Make a Comeback in Syria," *Atlantic*, September 18, 2018d.

———, "The True Origins of ISIS," *Atlantic*, November 30, 2018e. As of January 2, 2019:
https://www.theatlantic.com/ideas/archive/2018/11/isis-origins-anbari-zarqawi/577030/

———, "A Hollow Victory Over the Islamic State in Syria? The High Risk of Jihadi Revival in Deir ez-Zor's Euphrates River Valley," *CTC Sentinel*, Vol. 12, No. 2, February 2019, pp. 1–6. As of April 6, 2019:
https://ctc.usma.edu/
hollow-victory-islamic-state-syria-high-risk-jihadi-revival-deir-ez-zors-euphrates-river-valley/

Hegazy, Amgad, "Food and Electricity Subsidies in Iraq," in Koba Gvenetadze and Amgad Hegazy, *Iraq: Selected Issues*, Washington, D.C.: International Monetary Fund, Country Report No. 15/236, August 2015. As of May 22, 2019:
https://www.imf.org/external/pubs/ft/scr/2015/cr15236.pdf

Heißner, Stefan, Peter R. Neumann, John Holland-McCowan, and Rajan Basra, "Caliphate in Decline: An Estimate of Islamic State's Financial Fortunes," London: International Centre for the Study of Radicalisation, 2017. As of June 7, 2019:
https://icsr.info/wp-content/uploads/2017/02/
ICSR-Report-Caliphate-in-Decline-An-Estimate-of-Islamic-States-Financial-Fortunes.pdf

Hoffman, Bruce, *Inside Terrorism*, 2nd ed., New York: Columbia University Press, 2006.

Hunaidi, Sarah, "ISIS Has Not Been Defeated. It's Alive and Well in Southern Syria," *Foreign Policy*, April 3, 2019.

Hussein, Rikar, "Islamic State Regrouping in Iraqi, Kurdish Disputed Territories," VOA website, March 26, 2018. As of December 11, 2018:
https://www.voanews.com/a/
islamic-state-regrouping-in-iraqi-kurdish-disputed-territories/4317597.html

Ibrahim, Waleed, "Al Qaeda's Two Top Iraq Leaders Killed in Raid," Reuters, April 19, 2010. As of June 28, 2018:
https://www.reuters.com/article/us-iraq-violence-alqaeda/
al-qaedas-two-top-iraq-leaders-killed-in-raid-idUSTRE63I3CL20100419

IHS Markit, "Islamic State Monthly Revenue Drops to $56 Million, IHS Says," press release, April 18, 2016. As of December 10, 2018:
https://news.ihsmarkit.com/press-release/aerospace-defense-security/
islamic-state-monthly-revenue-drops-56-million-ihs-says

———, "Islamic State Territory Down 60 Percent and Revenue Down 80 Percent on Caliphate's Third Anniversary, IHS Markit Says," press release, June 29, 2017. As of April 24, 2018:
http://news.ihsmarkit.com/press-release/aerospace-defense-security/
islamic-state-territory-down-60-percent-and-revenue-down-80

Ingram, Haroro J., and Craig Whiteside, "The Caliph's Role in the (un)Surprising Resilience of the Islamic State," Foreign Policy Research Institute website, October 25, 2018. As of June 24, 2019:
https://www.fpri.org/article/2018/10/the-caliphs-role-in-the-unsurprising-resilience-of-the-islamic-state/

International Labour Organization, "Syrian Arab Republic," webpage, 2015. As of April 6, 2019:
https://www.ilo.org/gateway/faces/home/ctryHome?locale=EN&countryCode=SYR&_adf.ctrl-state=152lzg91xl_4

"Iraq Country Profile," BBC News website, October 3, 2018. As of December 10, 2018:
https://www.bbc.com/news/world-middle-east-14542954

"Iraq Takes Daesh's Biggest Financiers by Surprise . . . and Seizes from Them 500 Million Dollars [العراق يباغت أكبر ممولي داعش . . . ويحرمه من 500 مليون دولار]," *Sky News Arabia*, February 21, 2019.

Iraqi Organization for Women and Future and Kvinna, *Research Survey Report on More Safety to Al-Anbar Women Project with Decision (1325)*, Baghdad, Iraq, 2018.

"Islamic State Has Been Stashing Millions of Dollars in Iraq and Abroad," *Economist*, February 22, 2018. As of December 11, 2018:
https://www.economist.com/middle-east-and-africa/2018/02/22/islamic-state-has-been-stashing-millions-of-dollars-in-iraq-and-abroad

Johnston, Patrick B., "Countering ISIL's Financing," testimony presented before the House Financial Services Committee on November 13, 2014, Santa Monica, Calif.: RAND Corporation, CT-419, 2014. As of March 30, 2017:
https://www.rand.org/pubs/testimonies/CT419.html

———, "Islamic State's Money Problems," *USA Today*, March 4, 2016. As of April 24, 2018:
https://www.usatoday.com/story/opinion/2016/03/04/islamic-state-airstrikes-oil-prices-taxation-extortion-finances-syria-iraq-column/81207344/

Johnston, Patrick B., Jacob N. Shapiro, Howard J. Shatz, Benjamin Bahney, Danielle F. Jung, Patrick K. Ryan, and Jonathan Wallace, *Foundations of the Islamic State: Management, Money, and Terror in Iraq, 2005–2010*, Santa Monica, Calif.: RAND Corporation, RR-1192-DARPA, 2016. As of January 24, 2017:
http://www.rand.org/pubs/research_reports/RR1192.html

Jones, Sam, and Erika Solomon, "Isis Inc.: Jihadis Fund War Machine but Squeeze 'Citizens,'" *Financial Times*, December 15, 2015.

Jonsson, Michael, *Funding the Islamic State: Sources of Revenue, Financing Requirements and Long-Term Vulnerabilities to Counter-Measures*, Stockholm: Swedish Defense Research Agency, December 2015.

Joscelyn, Thomas, "Islamic State Rescinds One of Its Most Problematic Religious Rulings," *Long War Journal*, September 20, 2017.

Kadercan, Burak, "Territorial Logic of the Islamic State: An Interdisciplinary Approach," *Territory, Politics, Governance*, Vol. 7, No. 1, March 2019.

Kalyvas, Stathis N., *The Logic of Violence in Civil War*, New York: Cambridge University Press, 2006.

Karouny, Mariam, "Insight—Syria's Nusra Front May Leave Qaeda to Form New Entity," Reuters, March 4, 2015. As of May 3, 2017:
http://uk.reuters.com/article/uk-mideast-crisis-nusra-insight-idUKKBN0M00G620150304

Keatinge, Tom, "The Importance of Financing in Enabling and Sustaining the Conflict in Syria (and Beyond)," *Perspectives on Terrorism*, Vol. 8, No. 4, 2014. As of December 10, 2018:
http://www.terrorismanalysts.com/pt/index.php/pot/article/view/360

Keller, Andrew, "Documenting ISIL's Antiquities Trafficking: The Looting and Destruction of Iraqi and Syrian Cultural Heritage: What We Know and What Can be Done," remarks at the Metropolitan Museum of Art, New York, September 29, 2015. As of March 16, 2018:
https://2009-2017.state.gov/e/eb/rls/rm/2015/247610.htm

Kennedy, Merrit, "New Report Finds ISIS Territorial Defeats Are Also Hitting the Group's Wallet," National Public Radio, February 21, 2017. As of December 10, 2018:
https://www.npr.org/sections/thetwo-way/2017/02/21/516466023/new-report-finds-isis-territorial-defeats-are-also-hitting-the-groups-wallet

Kenner, David, "All ISIS Has Left Is Money. Lots of It," *Atlantic*, March 24, 2019. As of April 1, 2019:
https://www.theatlantic.com/international/archive/2019/03/isis-caliphate-money-territory/584911/

Kilcullen, David, *Blood Year: Islamic State and the Failure of the War on Terror*, London: Hurst and Company, 2016.

Knights, Michael, "Predicting the Shape of Iraq's Next Sunni Insurgencies," *CTC Sentinel*, Vol. 10, No. 7, August 2017, pp. 13–22. As of May 13, 2019:
https://ctc.usma.edu/predicting-the-shape-of-iraqs-next-sunni-insurgencies/

Kuntz, Katrin, "Sex Slave Legacy: The Children of the Islamic State," *Spiegel Online*, April 14, 2016.

Kurdistan Region Security Council, "Joint Op by our Counter Terrorism Dept (CTD) & U.S. Special forces killed snr #ISIL member near Iraqi-Syrian border," press release via Twitter, Office of the Chancellor, August 11, 2016. As of January 19, 2019:
https://twitter.com/KRSCPress/status/763715266769522689

Lead Inspector General for Overseas Contingency Operations, *Operation Inherent Resolve: Quarterly Report to the United States Congress, April 1, 2015–June 30, 2015*, August 24, 2015a.

———, *Operation Inherent Resolve: Quarterly Report and Biannual Report to the United States Congress, September 30, 2015*, December 3, 2015b.

———, *Operation Inherent Resolve: Quarterly Report to the United States Congress, March 31, 2016*, May 6, 2016.

———, *Operation Inherent Resolve: Quarterly Report to the United States Congress, October 1, 2016–December 31, 2016*, February 2, 2017a.

———, *Operation Inherent Resolve: Report to the United States Congress, July 1, 2017–September 30, 2017*, Washington, D.C., November 3, 2017b. As of December 11, 2018:
http://www.dodig.mil/Reports/Lead-Inspector-General-Reports/Article/1362065/lead-inspector-general-for-operation-inherent-resolve-quarterly-report-to-the-u/

———, *Operation Inherent Resolve and Operation Pacific Eagle—Philippines: Report to the United States Congress, October 1, 2017–December 31, 2017*, Washington, D.C., February 2, 2018.

Levitt, Matthew, "Terrorist Financing and the Islamic State," testimony submitted to the House Committee on Financial Services, November 13, 2014. As of April 25, 2018:
http://www.washingtoninstitute.org/policy-analysis/view/terrorist-financing-and-the-islamic-state

Lewis, Alexander, "Coalition Hopes to Use ISIL's Own Tax Regime Against It," Tax Notes International website, May 2, 2016.

Lewis, Bernard, *From Babel to Dragomans: Interpreting the Middle East*, New York: Oxford University Press, 2004.

Lister, Charles, "Profiling the Islamic State," Doha: Brookings Doha Center, Analysis Paper 13, November 2014.

Londoño, Ernesto, "No. 2 Leader of Al-Qaeda in Iraq Killed," *Washington Post*, October 16, 2008. As of January 24, 2019:
http://www.washingtonpost.com/wp-dyn/content/article/2008/10/15/AR2008101500682.html

Loveluck, Louisa, "Anger and Fear Along Turkey's Border as Offensive Brings the War Back Home," *Washington Post*, February 7, 2018. As of April 6, 2019:
https://www.washingtonpost.com/world/anger-and-fear-along-turkeys-border-as-offensive-brings-the-war-back-home/2018/02/06/7a310eec-0abf-11e8-998c-96deb18cca19_story.html?utm_term=.bd5417a4e2a8

Loveluck, Louisa, and Mustafa Salim, "Iraq's Prime Minister Announces Victory Against the Islamic State in Mosul," *Washington Post*, July 10, 2017. As of January 26, 2019:
https://www.washingtonpost.com/world/middle_east/iraqs-prime-minister-announces-victory-against-the-islamic-state-in-mosul/2017/07/10/28450c32-656a-11e7-94ab-5b1f0ff459df_story.html?utm_term=.79d78c30e938

Loveluck, Louisa, and Zakaria Zakaria, "Syria's Once-Teeming Prison Cells are Being Emptied by Mass Murder," *Washington Post*, December 23, 2018. As of January 28, 2019:
https://www.washingtonpost.com/graphics/2018/world/syria-bodies/?utm_term=.bdb48e11a84f

Lyall, Jason, and Isaiah Wilson III, "Rage Against the Machines: Explaining Outcomes in Counterinsurgency Wars," *International Organization*, Vol. 63, No. 1, 2009, pp. 67–106.

Mansour, Renad, and Hisham al-Hashimi, "ISIS and the New War Economy," Chatham House website, June 8, 2017. As of June 11, 2018:
https://www.chathamhouse.org/expert/comment/isis-and-new-war-economy

———, "ISIS Is Still in Business," Chatham House website, January 17, 2018. As of April 25, 2018:
https://www.chathamhouse.org/expert/comment/isis-still-business

al-Masri, Abu Abdullah, "Principles in the Administration of the Islamic State," trans. Aymenn Jawad Al-Tamimi, in "The Isis Papers: A Masterplan for Consolidating Power," *Guardian*, December 7, 2015. As of November 15, 2018:
https://www.theguardian.com/world/2015/dec/07/islamic-state-document-masterplan-for-power

McCoy, Terrence, "ISIS Just Stole $425 Million, Iraqi Governor Says, and Became the 'World's Richest Terrorist Group,'" *Washington Post*, June 12, 2014. As of April 24, 2018:
https://www.washingtonpost.com/news/morning-mix/wp/2014/06/12/isis-just-stole-425-million-and-became-the-worlds-richest-terrorist-group/

McGuinness, Romina, "ISIS Net Worth REVEALED: Islamic State Is Worth £2.6BILLION Despite Losses," *Express*, April 26, 2018. As of June 11, 2018:
https://www.express.co.uk/news/world/951754/ISIS-net-worth-revealed-how-much-is-Islamic-State-worth

Michaels, Jim, "U.S. Coalition Slashes ISIS Oil Revenue by More Than 90%," *USA Today*, October 2, 2017. As of May 13, 2019:
https://www.usatoday.com/story/news/world/2017/10/02/u-s-coalition-slashes-isis-oil-revenue-more-than-90/717303001/

Miklaszewski, Jim, and Corky Siemaszko, "Millions in ISIS Cash Destroyed in U.S. Airstrike," NBC News, January 11, 2016. As of January 19, 2019: https://www.nbcnews.com/storyline/isis-terror/millions-isis-cash-destroyed-u-s-airstrike-n494261

Moore, Jack, "U.S.-Led Coalition Targets ISIS Banks in Mosul Strikes," *Newsweek*, February 15, 2016. As of January 19, 2019: https://www.newsweek.com/us-led-coalition-targets-isis-banks-mosul-strikes-426604

———, "ISIS Members Plundered $800 Million From Iraq, Central Bank Says," *Newsweek*, August 9, 2017. As of March 17, 2018: http://www.newsweek.com/isis-members-plundered-800-million-iraq-central-bank-says-648492

Al-Najar, Kamaran, Patrick Osgood, and Staff, "Kurdish Troops Advance on Kirkuk," *Iraq Oil Report*, April 30, 2013.

"'New Baghdadi Tape' Posted by Islamic State Group," BBC News, September 29, 2017. As of December 11, 2018: https://www.bbc.com/news/world-middle-east-41435183

Noack, Rick, "Here's How the Islamic State Compares with Real States," *Washington Post*, September 12, 2014. As of April 25, 2018: https://www.washingtonpost.com/news/worldviews/wp/2014/09/12/heres-how-the-islamic-state-compares-to-real-states/

Nordland, Rod, "ISIS Fighters, Having Pledged to Fight or Die, Surrender en Masse," *New York Times*, October 8, 2017. As of December 11, 2018: https://www.nytimes.com/2017/10/08/world/middleeast/isis-iraq-surrender.html

O'Connor, Niall, "Gardai Raid 'ISIS Cash Gang' After Tip Off by Bank in Dublin," *Irish Mirror*, January 23, 2019. As of January 26, 2019: https://www.irishmirror.ie/news/irish-news/crime/gardai-raid-isis-cash-gang-13894468

O'Connor, Tom, "Donald Trump Says Saudi Arabia, Not 'Great Country' U.S., Will Rebuild Syria," *Newsweek*, December 24, 2018.

Olidort, Jacob, "What Is Salafism? How a Nonpolitical Ideology Became a Political Force," *Foreign Affairs*, November 24, 2015. As of January 30, 2017: https://www.foreignaffairs.com/articles/syria/2015-11-24/what-salafism

Pagliery, Jose, "ISIS Cuts Its Fighters' Salaries by 50%," CNN, January 19, 2016. As of April 6, 2019: https://money.cnn.com/2016/01/19/news/world/isis-salary-cuts/index.html

Pape, Robert A., *Dying to Win: The Strategic Logic of Suicide Terrorism*, New York: Random House, 2005.

Pellerin, Cheryl, "Inherent Resolve Spokesman: Coalition Operations Deny ISIL's Caliphate Dreams," DoD News website, May 13, 2016. As of June 7, 2019: https://www.inherentresolve.mil/Media-Library/News-Releases/Article/760921/inherent-resolve-spokesman-coalition-operations-deny-isils-caliphate-dreams/

———, "OIR Spokesman: No Safe Havens Left for ISIS in Syria or Iraq," DoD News website, August 10, 2017. As of January 19, 2019: http://www.centcom.mil/MEDIA/NEWS-ARTICLES/News-Article-View/Article/1275462/oir-spokesman-no-safe-havens-left-for-isis-in-syria-or-iraq/

Rasheed, Ahmed, "Islamic State's Oil Revenue Dives as It Loses Iraqi Territory," Reuters, July 28, 2016. As of June 24, 2019: http://www.reuters.com/article/us-mideast-crisis-iraq-oil-idUSKCN1081JI

Rasmussen, Sune Engel, and Nazih Osseiran, "Islamic State Kills Dozens of U.S.-Backed Fighters in Syria Battle, Monitor Says," *Wall Street Journal*, November 26, 2018. As of December 12, 2018: https://www.wsj.com/articles/islamic-state-kills-dozens-of-u-s-backed-fighters-in-syria-battle-monitor-says-1543255710

Reed, Matthew, "Blowing Up the Islamic State's Oil Company," *Foreign Policy*, October 26, 2016. As of April 24, 2018: https://foreignpolicy.com/2016/10/26/blowing-up-the-islamic-states-oil-company-isis-abu-sayyaf/

———, "ISIS Is Out of the Oil Business," *Fuse*, March 27, 2018. As of April 24, 2018: http://energyfuse.org/isis-oil-business/

"Remaining and Expanding," *Dabiq*, No. 5, Muharram 1436 [October–November 2014].

"The Revival of Slavery Before the Hour," *Dabiq*, No. 4, Dhul-Hijjah 1435 [September–October 2014].

Ricks, Thomas E., and Karen DeYoung, "Al-Qaeda in Iraq Reported Crippled," *Washington Post*, October 15, 2007. As of June 28, 2018: http://www.washingtonpost.com/wp-dyn/content/article/2007/10/14/AR2007101401245.html

Riley, Charles, "ISIS Is Losing Mosul and Most of Its Income," CNN Money website, June 29, 2017. As of December 10, 2018: http://money.cnn.com/2017/06/29/news/isis-finances-territory/index.html

Robinson, Eric, Daniel Egel, Patrick B. Johnston, Sean Mann, Alexander D. Rothenberg, and David Stebbins, *When the Islamic State Comes to Town: The Economic Impact of Islamic State Governance in Iraq and Syria*, Santa Monica, Calif.: RAND Corporation, RR-1970-RC, 2017. As of June 28, 2018: https://www.rand.org/pubs/research_reports/RR1970.html

Roggio, Bill, "Al Qaeda in Iraq's Second in Command Was a Swedish Citizen," *Long War Journal*, October 16, 2008. As of January 24, 2019: https://www.longwarjournal.org/archives/2008/10/al_qaeda_in_iraqs_se.php

Rosenberg, Matthew, "U.S. Drops Bombs Not Just on ISIS, But on Its Cash, Too," *New York Times*, January 20, 2016. As of April 24, 2018: https://www.nytimes.com/2016/01/21/us/politics/us-drops-bombs-not-just-on-isis-but-on-its-cash-too.html

Salama, Basma, *The Resilience of the Islamic State*, Republik Österreich: Bundesministerium für Landesverteidigung und Sport, 2016. As of December 10, 2018: http://www.bundesheer.at/pdf_pool/publikationen/resilience_of_islamic_state_b_salama.pdf

Samer, *The Raqqa Diaries: Escape from the Islamic State*, ed. Mike Thompson, illus. Scott Coelho, Interlink Pub Group, 2017.

Shapiro, Jacob N., "A Predictable Failure: The Political Economy of the Decline of the Islamic State," *CTC Sentinel*, Vol. 9, No. 9, September 2016, pp. 28–32.

Shapiro, Jacob N., and Janet Hansen-Lewis, "Understanding the Daesh Economy," *Perspectives on Terrorism*, Vol. 9, No. 4, August 2015, pp. 142–155.

Shatz, Howard J., and Erin-Elizabeth Johnson, *The Islamic State We Knew: Insights Before the Resurgence and Their Implications*, Santa Monica, Calif.: RAND Corporation, RR-1267-OSD, 2015. As of March 30, 2017: https://www.rand.org/pubs/research_reports/RR1267.html

SITE Institute, "Islamic State of Iraq Announces Establishment of the Cabinet of its First Islamic Administration in Video Issued Through al-Furqan Foundation," April 19, 2007. As of February 7, 2017: https://web.archive.org/web/20070928061225/http://www.siteinstitute.org/bin/articles.cgi?ID=publications274907&Category=publications&Subcategory=0

Sly, Liz, and Louisa Loveluck, "The 'Caliphate' Is No More. But the Islamic State Isn't Finished Yet," *Washington Post*, March 23, 2019. As of April 8, 2019: https://www.washingtonpost.com/world/the-islamic-states-caliphate-has-been-defeated-us-backed-forces-say/2019/03/23/04263d74-36f8-11e9-8375-e3dcf6b68558_story.html?utm_term=.d025fe2f7cc7

Solomon, Erika, "The ISIS Economy: Meet the New Boss," *The Financial Times*, January 5, 2015. As of April 6, 2019: https://www.ft.com/content/b2c6b5ca-9427-11e4-82c7-00144feabdc0

Solomon, Erika, Guy Chazan, and Sam Jones, "ISIS Inc.: How Oil Fuels the Jihadi Terrorists," *Financial Times*, October 14, 2015.

Solomon, Erika, and Sam Jones, "ISIS Inc.: Loot and Taxes Keep Jihadi Economy Churning," *Financial Times*, December 14, 2015.

Solomon, Erika, and Ahmed Mhidi, "ISIS Inc.: Syria's 'Mafia-Style' Gas Deals with Jihadis," *Financial Times*, October 15, 2015. As of April 6, 2019: https://www.ft.com/content/92f4e036-6b69-11e5-aca9-d87542bf8673

"Specimen 12Q: Lowering of Salaries for Fighters by 50%," in Al-Tamimi, 2016a.

"Specimen 14U: Salary Scheme Table for Al Bara' bin Malek Battalion Members," from Al-Tamimi, 2016a.

"Specimen 15O: Expenses Request for a Battalion in Sha'aban 1436 AH, Homes Province," from Al-Tamimi, 2016a.

"Specimen 17N: Personnel List: Fallujah Area," from Al-Tamimi, 2016a.

"Specimen 17O: Personnel List: Fallujah Area (Cont.)," from Al-Tamimi, 2016a.

"Specimen 18N: Financial Data on Payments to Personnel in Anbar for Safr 1436 AH," from Al-Tamimi, 2016a.

"Specimen 19N: Personnel List: Homs," from Al-Tamimi, 2016a.

"Specimen 33K: Monthly Expenses for an Islamic State Squadron in Aleppo Province" from Al-Tamimi, 2016d.

"Specimen 33N: Personnel List from Battalion 57, Aleppo Province," from Al-Tamimi, 2016d.

"Specimen K: Employment Opportunities with Diwan al-Hisbah, Raqqa Province," from Al-Tamimi, 2015a.

Strack, Columb, "Islamic State Territory Shrinks by 9.4% in First Six Months of 2015," *Jane's Intelligence Review*, July 28, 2015. As of April 3, 2019: https://www.janes.com/article/53239/islamic-state-territory-shrinks-by-9-4-in-first-six-months-of-2015

"Syria Country Profile," BBC, April 24, 2018. As of December 10, 2018: https://www.bbc.com/news/world-middle-east-14703856

Szubin, Adam, "Remarks by Acting Under Secretary Adam Szubin at Chatham House," Washington, D.C.: U.S. Department of the Treasury, December 10, 2015. As of December 10, 2018: https://www.treasury.gov/press-center/press-releases/Pages/jl0299.aspx

———, "Remarks of Acting Under Secretary Adam Szubin on Countering the Financing of Terrorism at the Paul H. Nitze School of Advanced International Studies," Washington, D.C.: U.S. Department of the Treasury, October 20, 2016. As of January 19, 2019: https://www.treasury.gov/press-center/press-releases/Pages/jl0590.aspx

Al-Tamimi, Aymenn Jawad, "Archive of Islamic State Administrative Documents," webpage, January 27, 2015a. As of January 24, 2019: http://www.aymennjawad.org/2015/01/archive-of-islamic-state-administrative-documents

———, "The Evolution in Islamic State Administration: The Documentary Evidence," *Perspectives on Terrorism*, Vol. 9, No. 4, October 2015b, pp. 117–129.

———, "Archive of Islamic State Administrative Documents (cont.)," webpage, January 11, 2016a. As of January 24, 2019:
http://www.aymennjawad.org/2016/01/archive-of-islamic-state-administrative-documents-1

———, "A Caliphate Under Strain: The Documentary Evidence," *CTC Sentinel*, Vol. 9, No. 4, April 2016b, pp. 1–8. As of April 6, 2019:
https://ctc.usma.edu/a-caliphate-under-strain-the-documentary-evidence/

———, "Al-Qa'ida Uncoupling: Jabhat Al-Nusra's Rebranding as Jabhat Fateh Al-Sham," *CTC Sentinel*, Vol. 9, No. 8, August 22, 2016c. As of February 7, 2017:
https://www.ctc.usma.edu/posts/al-qaida-uncoupling-jabhat-al-nusras-rebranding-as-jabhat-fateh-al-sham

———, "Archive of Islamic State Administrative Documents (continued . . . again)," webpage, September 17, 2016d. As of January 24, 2019:
http://www.aymennjawad.org/2016/09/archive-of-islamic-state-administrative-documents-2

———, "Archive of Islamic State Administrative Documents (cont.—IV)," webpage, August 28, 2017. As of January 24, 2019:
http://www.aymennjawad.org/2016/09/archive-of-islamic-state-administrative-documents-3

Taub, Ben, "Iraq's Post-ISIS Campaign of Revenge," *New Yorker*, December 24, 2018.

Tezcür, Güneş Murat, "Three Years Ago, the Islamic State Massacred Yazidis in Iraq. Why?" *Washington Post*, August 15, 2017. As of January 25, 2019:
https://www.washingtonpost.com/news/monkey-cage/wp/2017/08/15/three-years-ago-the-islamic-state-massacred-yazidis-in-iraq-why/?utm_term=.f8437f2a2335

Torbati, Yeganeh, "Islamic State Yearly Oil Revenue Halved to $250 Million: U.S. Official," Reuters, May 11, 2016. As of December 12, 2018:
https://www.reuters.com/article/us-mideast-crisis-islamic-state-revenue-idUSKCN0Y22CW

"Unifying the Ranks," *Dabiq*, No. 5, Muharram 1436 [October–November 2014].

United Nations, "In ISIL-Controlled Territory, 8 Million Civilians Living In 'State of Fear'—UN Expert," UN News website, July 31, 2015a. As of April 7, 2019:
https://news.un.org/en/story/2015/07/505512-isil-controlled-territory-8-million-civilians-living-state-fear-un-expert

———, "Security Council Unanimously Adopts Resolution 2254 (2015), Endorsing Road Map for Peace Process in Syria, Setting Timetables for Talks," SC/12171, December 18, 2015b. As of January 28, 2019: https://www.un.org/press/en/2015/sc12171.doc.htm

United Nations Development Program, *Iraq Human Development Report 2014: Iraqi Youth: Challenges and Opportunities*, Iraq: Ministry of Planning and Bayt al Hikma, 2014.

United Nations Security Council, Resolution 2170, August 15, 2014a. As of January 26, 2019: http://www.un.org/en/ga/search/view_doc.asp?symbol=S/RES/2170%20(2014)

———, Letter Dated 13 November 2014 from the Chair of the Security Council Committee Pursuant to Resolutions 1267 (1999) and 1989 (2011) Concerning Al-Qaida and Associated Individuals and Entities Addressed to the President of the Security Council, S/2014/815, November 14, 2014b.

———, Resolution 2253, December 17, 2015. As of June 1, 2019: https://www.un.org/en/ga/search/view_doc.asp?symbol=S/RES/2253%282015%29

———, *Twenty-Second Report of the Analytical Support and Sanctions Monitoring Team Submitted Pursuant to Resolution 2368 (2017) Concerning ISIL (Da'esh), Al-Qaida and Associated Individuals and Entities*, S/2018/705, New York, July 27, 2018.

———, *Eighth Report of the Secretary-General on the Threat Posed by ISIL (Da'esh) to International Peace and Security and the Range of United Nations Efforts in Support of Member States in Countering the Threat*, February 1, 2019.

University of Pennsylvania, Exchange Rate to U.S. Dollar for Syria [FXRATESYA618NUPN], retrieved from FRED, Federal Reserve Bank of St. Louis, updated September 17, 2012. As of April 6, 2019: https://fred.stlouisfed.org/series/FXRATESYA618NUPN

UNSC—*See* United Nations Security Council.

U.S. Census, International Data Base, rev. September 18, 2018. As of April 7, 2019: https://www.census.gov/programs-surveys/international-programs/about/idb.html

U.S. Central Command, "Military Airstrikes Continue Against ISIL Terrorists in Syria and Iraq," press release, June 23, 2016. As of January 19, 2019: http://www.centcom.mil/MEDIA/PRESS-RELEASES/Press-Release-View/Article/904640/june-23-military-airstrikes-continue-against-isil-terrorists-in-syria-and-iraq/

U.S. Department of State, Country Reports on Terrorism 2005, Washington, D.C.: Office of the Coordinator for Counterterrorism, April 2006.

———, "The Global Coalition—Working to Defeat ISIS," fact sheet, Washington, D.C.: Office of the Spokesperson, March 22, 2017. As of January 19, 2019:
https://www.state.gov/the-global-coalition-working-to-defeat-isis/

U.S. Department of the Treasury, "Treasury Designates Twelve Foreign Terrorist Fighter Facilitators," press release, Washington, D.C., September 24, 2014.

———, "United States, Italy, and the Kingdom of Saudi Arabia Hold Fourth Plenary of the Counter-ISIL Finance Group in Rome," press release, Washington, D.C., April 11, 2016a. As of January 19, 2019:
https://www.treasury.gov/press-center/press-releases/Pages/jl0416.aspx

———, "Treasury Sanctions Senior ISIL Financier and Two Money Service Businesses," press release, Washington, D.C., December 13, 2016b.

———, "Treasury Sanctions Iraq-Based ISIS Financial Facilitation Network," press release, Washington, D.C., June 15, 2017.

———, *National Terrorist Financing Risk Assessment*, Washington, D.C., 2018a.

———, "Treasury Targets Iraq-Based Money Service Business Supporting ISIS," press release, Washington, D.C., October 17, 2018b.

Van Ostaeyen, Pieter, "Pietervanostaeyn: Musings on Arabism, Islamicism, History, and Current Affairs," website, undated.

Wagemakers, Joas, "Invoking Zarqawi: Abu Muhammad al-Maqdisi's Jihad Deficit," *CTC Sentinel*, Vol. 2, No. 6, June 2009. As of June 10, 2019:
https://ctc.usma.edu/app/uploads/2010/06/Vol2Iss6-Art5.pdf

Warren, Steve, "Department of Defense Press Briefing by Col. Warren," Operation Inherent Resolve Spokesman, December 10, 2015.

Warrick, Joby, *Black Flags: The Rise of ISIS*, New York: Anchor, 2015.

———, "Satellite Photos Show Islamic State Installing Hundreds of Makeshift Oil Refineries to Offset Losses from Airstrikes," *Washington Post*, July 7, 2016. As of April 24, 2018:
https://www.washingtonpost.com/news/worldviews/wp/2016/07/07/satellite-photos-show-isis-installing-hundreds-of-makeshift-oil-refineries-to-offset-losses-from-air-strikes/

———, "Retreating ISIS Army Smuggled a Fortune in Cash and Gold Out of Iraq and Syria," *Washington Post*, December 21, 2018.

Warrick, Joby, Will McCants, and Aaron Y. Zelin, "The Rise of ISIS: 'Remaining and Expanding,'" Washington Institute for Near East Policy, PolicyWatch 2522, November 12, 2015. As of February 8, 2017:
http://www.washingtoninstitute.org/policy-analysis/view/the-rise-of-isis-remaining-and-expanding

Warrick, Joby, and Liz Sly, "U.S.-Led Strikes Putting a Financial Squeeze on the Islamic State," *Washington Post*, April 2, 2016. As of April 24, 2018: https://www.washingtonpost.com/world/national-security/us-led-strikes-putting-a-financial-squeeze-on-the-islamic-state/2016/04/02/e739a7be-f848-11e5-a3ce-f06b5ba21f33_story.html

Weinberg, David Andrew, *Qatar and Terror Finance Part II: Private Funders of al-Qaeda in Syria*, Washington, D.C.: Foundation for Defense of Democracies, January 2017.

Weiss, Michael, "Leaked ISIS Documents Show Internal Chaos," *Daily Beast*, August 30, 2016.

Weiss, Michael, and Hassan Hassan, "How to Salvage Syria," *Daily Beast*, December 7, 2016. As of January 28, 2019: https://www.thedailybeast.com/how-to-salvage-syria

White House, "Fact Sheet: Strategy to Counter the Islamic State of Iraq and the Levant (ISIL)," Washington, D.C.: Office of the Press Secretary, September 10, 2014. As of January 26, 2019: https://obamawhitehouse.archives.gov/the-press-office/2014/09/10/fact-sheet-strategy-counter-islamic-state-iraq-and-levant-isil

Whiteside, Craig, "War, Interrupted, Part I: The Roots of the Jihadist Resurgence in Iraq," War on the Rocks website, November 5, 2014a. As of January 26, 2019: https://warontherocks.com/2014/11/war-interrupted-part-i-the-roots-of-the-jihadist-resurgence-in-iraq/

———, "War, Interrupted, Part II: From Prisoners to Rulers," War on the Rocks website, November 6, 2014b. As of January 26, 2019: https://warontherocks.com/2014/11/war-interrupted-part-ii-from-prisoners-to-rulers/

———, "ISIL's Small Ball Warfare: An Effective Way to Get Back Into the Game," War on the Rocks website, April 29, 2015. As of June 24, 2019: https://warontherocks.com/2015/04/isils-small-ball-warfare-an-effective-way-to-get-back-into-a-ballgame/

———, "The Islamic State and the Return of Revolutionary Warfare," *Small Wars & Insurgencies*, Vol. 27, No. 5, August 2016a, pp. 743–776.

———, "New Masters of Revolutionary Warfare: The Islamic State Movement (2002–2016)," *Perspectives on Terrorism*, Vol. 10, No. 4, August 2016b, pp. 6–20.

———, "Nine Bullets for the Traitors, One for the Enemy: The Slogans and Strategy Behind the Islamic State's Campaign to Defeat the Sunni Awakening (2006–2017)," The Hague: International Centre for Counter-Terrorism, September 2018.

Williams, Heather J., Nathan Chandler, and Eric Robinson, *Trends in the Draw of Americans to Foreign Terrorist Organizations from 9/11 to Today*, Santa Monica, Calif.: RAND Corporation, RR-2545-OSD, 2018. As of January 2, 2019: https://www.rand.org/pubs/research_reports/RR2545.html

Windrem, Robert, "ISIS Is the World's Richest Terror Group, But Spending Money Fast," CNBC, March 20, 2015. As of January 21, 2019: https://www.cnbc.com/2015/03/20/isis-the-worlds-richest-terror-group-is-spending-money-fast.html

Wing, Joel, "Who Was Al Qaeda in Iraq's Abu Omar al-Baghdadi? Interview with Naval War College's Prof Craig Whiteside," Musings on Iraq website, June 13, 2016. As of February 8, 2017: http://musingsoniraq.blogspot.com/2016/06/who-was-al-qaeda-in-iraqs-abu-omar-al.html

Winter, Charlie, "War by Suicide: A Statistical Analysis of the Islamic State's Martyrdom Industry," The Hague: International Centre for Counter-Terrorism, February 2017. As of December 12, 2018: https://icct.nl/wp-content/uploads/2017/02/ICCT-Winter-War-by-Suicide-Feb2017.pdf

Woertz, Eckart, "How Long Will ISIS Last Economically?" Barcelona Centre for International Affairs, Notes Internacionals CIDOB No. 98, October 2014. As of December 10, 2018: https://www.cidob.org/en/publications/publication_series/notes_internacionals/n1_98/how_long_will_isis_last_economically

Yahya, Maha, "The Politics of Dispossession," Diwan, Carnegie Middle East Center, May 9, 2018.

Youssef, Nancy A., and Raja Abdulrahim, "At Least Four Americans Killed in Syria Attack Claimed by the United States," *Wall Street Journal*, January 16, 2019.

Zalloom, Abdul-Qadeem, *Funds in the Khilafah State*: *Al-Amwal fi Dowlat Al-Khilafah*, 2nd ed., London: Al-Khilafah Publications, May 1988.

Zelin, Aaron Y., "The Clairvoyant: Boko Haram's Media and The Islamic State Connection?" *Jihadology*, January 27, 2015a. As of March 17, 2018: http://jihadology.net/2015/01/27/the-clairvoyant-boko-harams-media-and-the-islamic-state-connection/

———, "Between the Islamic State and al-Qaeda in Tunisia," Washington Institute for Near East Policy, May 11, 2015b. As of March 17, 2018: http://www.washingtoninstitute.org/policy-analysis/view/between-the-islamic-state-and-al-qaeda-in-tunisia